rea3ons
WHY CHRISTIANS GO TO COUNSELING

John T. Cocoris, Th.M., Psy.D.

3 Reasons Christians Go To Counseling
©2015 By Dr. John T. Cocoris

All rights reserved. No part of this book may be reproduced in any form, except for the inclusion of brief quotations in a review, without permission in writing from the author:

John T. Cocoris
7209 Verdi Way
McKinney, TX 75070
(972) 529-9150

johncocoris@sbcglobal.net
www.fourtemperaments.com

ISBN   978-0-9721650-4-4
Library of Congress Card Number:

Profile Dynamics
McKinney, Texas 75070

Cover and interior design by April Beltran

acknowledgments

A NOTE OF THANKS

I am indebted to my brother, Mike Cocoris, who has read and edited the manuscript making helpful suggestions. I would also like to thank my wife, Darrellene Cocoris, for her helpful suggestions. Thanks also to my long time friend, Lane Hedgepeth, for editing the manuscript and offering valuable insights. A special thanks to April Beltran who read and edited the manuscript, offering insightful suggestions that has made this work better. April is also responsible for the interior layout and the book cover design.

table of contents

INTRODUCTION 1

PART ONE: TRIALS 3

    01. "Life is what happens while you're busy making other plans" 5
    02. The purpose of trials 9
    03. How to respond to trials 13
    04. Incorrect responses to trials 23
    05. Consequences of incorrect responses to trials 35

PART TWO: RELATIONSHIPS 39

    06. Relationship struggles 41
    07. Treat others the way God treats you 47

PART THREE: MENTAL DISORDERS 59

    08. Do I have a mental disorder? The medical model 61
    09. Do I have a mental disorder? Environmental Influences 73
    10. The Biblical view of behavior 77
    11. The Temperament Model of Behavior 87

PART FOUR: THE SPIRITUAL LIFE 93

    12. The spiritual life and counseling 95
    13. Why is the spiritual life so hard? 97
    14. Desire 99
    15. Voluntarily Obey 105
    16. Do not be conformed to this world 109
    17. Renew your mind 115
    18. Depend on the Holy Spirit 125
    19. Transformation 127
    20. Let God be God 129

CONCLUSION 133

ABOUT THE AUTHOR 135

REFERENCES 137

introduction

THE WHYS

Why do some Christians fall apart when life's circumstances overwhelm them? Why do some Christians get anxious, angry and depressed when life takes a painful turn? Why do some Christians have difficulties in relationships and even get divorced? Why do some Christians think they have a mental disorder?

To find answers to these and other troublesome questions, some Christians turn to Psychology for direction and others turn to Psychiatry for medication to help them cope with their circumstances. It is my belief that neither field has the answers that Christians need.

Over the years, I noticed that Christians seek counseling mostly for one of three reasons: trials, relationships or because they have been told they have a mental disorder. This book is not meant to be a treatment of every reason a person seeks counseling but only to discuss these three common reasons and offer Biblical answers.

After years of being a counselor, I found that Christians do not always respond well to what God says about their dilemma. Those coming for counseling fall into one of three categories; they do not know what God has said, they do not understand what God has said, or they do not care what God has said. But all come because they are not doing what God said. Not caring or doing what God said was inherited from Adam; he knew and understood what God said, but he just did not care.

I do not know the problem you may be facing but I do know that God has the answer. Seek the wisdom you need in His Word and choose to do what He says. Without individuals submitting themselves to obeying the Word of God, and the renewing work of the Holy Spirit, there is no hope for inner peace or lasting change. The answer to why we all have problems in life and what to do about it, is what this book is about. I trust that you will be enlightened as you read it and find the answers for which you are seeking.

John T. Cocoris
McKinney, Texas
Proverbs 3:5-6

part one
TRIALS

one

"LIFE IS WHAT HAPPENS WHILE YOU'RE BUSY MAKING OTHER PLANS"

This statement first appeared in 1957 in *Reader's Digest* credited to Allen Saunders. This profound and poetic truth identifies what we have all experienced--life is seemingly rolling along just fine when it suddenly makes a sharp, unexpected turn for the worse. We ask, *"Why me? why now? why this?"*

We have spouse problems and problems with our children. Some have suddenly lost their mate or their job. Houses burn down, serious car accidents happen, and many go through divorce. Everyone has had a bad day, bad week, bad month, bad year or longer, when everything just fell apart. Here are a few examples:

ONE AFTER ANOTHER

Have you ever had one of those days, maybe even weeks where it seems as if the infamous Murphy's Law (anything that can go wrong, will) only applied to you? Well me too. It all started for me and my wife on a Saturday morning. It appeared to be like any other Saturday until I opened the door to the garage. I could not believe my eyes. To my shock and disbelief, I saw the garage door laying on top of our cars. It had somehow collapsed during the night!

As soon as we got everything back to normal, we made a quick trip to Florida. About half way there our car engine suddenly stopped, and of course it was in a small town and on a weekend. We had to have the car towed to the dealer and rent a car. We were told there would be no problem fixing the car and it would be ready Monday morning. We drove back on Sunday so we could pick the car up as promised on Monday morning. And as luck would have it, the mechanic informed us that it actually won't be ready until Tuesday or Wednesday because the new part had not arrived.

I asked, "Where is the part coming from?" Would you believe it was in the town we had just left a few hundred miles away! So we quickly decided we would get the part ourselves so the car can get fixed.

When we finally returned home, I found that my computer had crashed-- yep dead as a doornail. That same week, I broke my little toe and soon after that, a knot the size of a golf ball suddenly appeared on my knee; still don't know what caused that.

There's more! Shortly after my knee made me look like an alien, I was driving on a freeway minding my own business when I looked up and said, "Are you kidding me?" A tire had fallen off of a flat-bed trailer and was rolling toward me. What do I do? Slow down, speed up, turn left or right? All of that was speeding through my mind as fast as the tire was approaching. By the way, some other object had fallen off the truck and it too was headed at me. I'm not sure how they both missed me, but they did! Things settled down for about a week when it started up again. The transmission in my car went out and it had to be replaced. Things like this never happen when you have money, right?

During that same week we heard strange noises coming out of our attic. Never did find out what that was. And then, our cat had his tail pulled so badly that it caused his vertebrate to separate. We kept him alive for nine months and finally had to have him put down. One disturbing event after another after another and it seemed to us that it would never stop.

BLINDSIDED

While there are trials composed of several inconvenient breakdowns, there are others where one blow is enough to completely knock us down. My brother, Mike, lives in Santa Monica, California. He had an appointment with a dentist to have his teeth cleaned and on that day he decided to walk to the office instead of driving. It was not that far from his home and the weather was providing another great day in southern California.

Before the dentist began he asked Mike how he was feeling. Mike said, "I am not feeling well." After some discussion the dentist decided that he should return home and they would do the procedure another day. Mike called a cab. By the time he got home he knew something was seriously wrong. He called his wife to take him to the hospital. The incident started around three in the afternoon and by six that evening he was unable to walk. He felt some tingling but he could not move his legs. The test revealed he had a tumor on his spinal cord between his shoulder blades. We all feared it would be cancer.

He was operated on the next day to remove the growth. It turned out to an abscess, not cancer, that was caused by a staph infection. It was not life threatening but it did substantially alter his life. He was told he would likely never walk again. If he was to gain any mobility back it was going to take years of physical therapy.

Why would such a thing happen to my brother, he is a pastor and devoted to the study and explanation of the Scripture?

THE UNTHINKABLE

Finally, there are those trials that are so devastating that moving on can seem utterly impossible.

Right after I started consulting with a company, the CEO called to ask if I would meet with the president that had just lost his son to an accident. The grief-stricken father told me that his 12 year old son was caring for a small calf for a school project. Every morning the boy would get up early to tend to the calf before preparing for school. The boy went out to the barn that morning to tend to the calf as he had been doing for a few months. It was always routine and uneventful. This time it was different.

The calf had a rope around it's neck so it would not run out of the barn. No one knows for sure what happened, but apparently the calf was spooked and went wild. The young boy tried to contain the calf but was not strong enough. By the time it was over, the calf had wrapped the rope numerous times around the young boy cutting off his ability to breathe. It happened so quickly he could not get away. The parents were committed and faithful Christians. They were active in their church.

One couple lost one of their twin daughters to a drowning accident. They had a backyard swimming pool and enjoyed family time with their twin girls. They were always very careful to supervise their five year old girls when outside in or near the pool. One day, the mother was working in the flower garden and had her back turned to the swimming pool. She did not see her daughter get into the pool and slip under the water. At least five minutes had passed before the mother noticed one of her girls was missing. When she saw her at the bottom of the pool she dove in to get her but it was too late and the child could not be revived.

I am writing this the morning after an ice storm moved through our area. I paused to look out the window and noticed there was so much ice clinging to the branches of our tree in the front yard that they were unable to hold the weight and were sagging, some to the point of almost breaking. Many have felt that way with the weight of the painful difficulties they are facing.

Trouble always raises questions. Why do these things happen? Why do seemingly bad things happen to Christians? When I realized what the Scripture said about the difficulties we experience, big or small, life finally made sense.

two

THE PURPOSE OF TRIALS

To understand trials and all that happens on your journey, you need to understand the purpose of the Christian life. Some have told me that the purpose of the Christian life is to serve God, share the Gospel, go to church, etc. While these are things we all need to do, they do not identify the purpose of the Christian life. So what exactly *is* God doing in your life?

TO BE CONFORMED INTO HIS IMAGE

The purpose of the Christian life is found in Romans 8:28-29. First, we need to understand the context in which verses 28-29 appear. Paul opens the paragraph in Romans 8:18 by stating, *"For I consider that the sufferings of this present time are not worthy to be compared with the glory which shall be revealed in us."* So Paul is going to explain why we suffer.

> **ROMANS 8:28-29**
> *And we know that all things work together for good to those who love God, to those who are the called according to His purpose. For whom He foreknew, He also predestined to be conformed to the image of His Son, that He might be the firstborn among many brethren.*

Now, let's unpack Romans 8:28 and 29 to find the answer. Paul states that "all things *work together*" for something he calls *good*. Notice that Paul did not say that all things in and of themselves are good, he said that all things work together toward something that he calls good. The good is identified in verse 29 when he says that *"For whom He foreknew* [Christians] *He also predestined to be conformed to the image of his Son."* The working of all things together create something called good, this "good" is us being conformed into the image of Jesus Christ. The purpose, therefore, of the Christian life is to be conformed into the image of His Son.

These two verses are teaching that God does not do anything TO you, He does it FOR you. All that happens in your life is designed to conform you into the image of Christ. God wants you to be like Him. That means God wants you to act like Jesus Christ and possess the qualities that He possesses. The fruit of the Spirit embodies what He wants you to be. Galatians 5:22-23 states, *"But the fruit of the Spirit is love, joy, peace, long-suffering, kindness, goodness, faithfulness, gentleness, self-control. Against such there is no law."* God wants you to show these qualities in your daily life.

Whatever you may be going through right now, big or small, has the divine purpose of molding you into the image of Jesus Christ. Here is what my brother, Mike, wrote in his book, *The Spiritual Life, Clarifying The Confusion About Being Conformed into the Image of Christ*:

> Thus far, I have described the nature of the spiritual life as a process of growing to Christ-like maturity in the context of a spiritual community. In other words, the goal of the spiritual life is Christ-like maturity. The question becomes, "What is Christ-like maturity?" Being God, Christ is holy and love. When He walked on this earth as a human, He was full of grace and truth. He was meek and gentle. He was submissive and had a servant's heart.
>
> That is only the beginning. The New Testament contains several lists of virtues believers need to develop (Gal. 5:22-23; 2 Cor. 6:4-10; 1 Tim. 6:11; Rev. 2:19). The items in these lists are characteristics of Christ-like maturity. Second Peter 1:5-7 is one of those lists that should be carefully considered.

God's chosen method to conform us into His image is pain and suffering through trials. It is only in our pain and suffering that we learn of God's grace, provision, and peace. It is only in our pain and suffering that we learn to know Him and to depend upon Him.

TOOTHPICKS OR HOUSES?

A man was casually walking down a small path on the river bank when he noticed a man standing at the end of a pier. He stopped to observe what he was doing. It was a bit puzzling to the traveler because he appeared to be separating logs as they were floating down the river. He had a long pole with a hook on the end and was using it to push some of the logs out into the main stream and others he would pull into a small cove next to the pier. His actions seemed to be random and without purpose. His curiosity drove him to ask the man just what he was up to. He walked out on the pier and said, "Excuse me sir but what exactly are you doing?" The older gentleman paused and said, "Well, some of the logs are good for building houses so I'm pushing them out into the main stream so they will be carried to the mill." "What about the other ones" he asked? The worker replied, "Well those are only good for making toothpicks, so I'm separating them to the side." Now the traveler's curiosity was even greater and he asked the obvious question, "And just how do you know the difference?" The old worker look at him and said, "When you've done this as long as I have, you can tell which trees were raised on the mountain tops and which ones were raised in the valley." He then explained, "The ones that were raised in the valley are not much good because they have not been exposed to the wind and they are not strong enough to be used for houses. They could only be used for toothpicks. Now the ones that were raised on the top of the mountain were subjected to the strong winds and were made strong enough to be used to build houses."

The only way to grow to maturity is through experiencing the punishing winds of life which will make us strong and useful. The former coach of the Dallas Cowboys Tom Landry was reported to have said, "We learn out of our failures not out of our successes." Imagine if your life went smoothly and you were able to get everything you wanted when you wanted it, you had plenty of money, you never got sick, and your family and friends prospered. Would you need God for anything?

If you were protected from the winds of life, you would never learn to be strong by trusting the Lord. It is only through adversity that we learn that God's grace is sufficient. Every Christian's purpose for living is for God to mold in us the characteristics of Jesus Christ. So remember, when storms and winds move into your life, big or small, God is not doing anything TO you, He is doing it FOR you so you will become like Jesus Christ.

STOP LOOKING FOR WHO'S AT FAULT

Christians often blame someone or something for the difficulties they experience. We inherited that idea from Adam. The first thing Adam did after he sinned was shift the blame for what he had done to God and the woman that God had given him (Genesis 3:12).

I am not saying that we always bring difficulty into our lives (although sometimes we do), I am saying that everyone has a tendency to point a finger at someone or something for which to blame their misfortune. We often rationalize just as Adam did that the blame has to put somewhere rather than accept the reality of the situation. We blame our spouse, our boss, the kids, circumstances, the weather, the neighbor's dog or cat, etc. to explain why we are experiencing difficulty. We reason that if it were not for this or that then we would not have this problem.

Never lose sight of the fact that whatever you are going through (big or small) is designed to teach you something about Jesus Christ. Never look beyond the truth that God is conforming you into the image of His Son through your current circumstances. Always remember that He is not doing anything *to* you, He is doing it *for* you. The Contemporary English Version (CEV) of the following two verse reflects the same truth that Paul is saying in Romans 8:28-29:

> **1 PETER 2:21**
> *After all, God chose you to suffer as you follow in the footsteps of Christ, who set an example by suffering for you.*
>
> **1 JOHN 2:6**
> *If we say we are his, we must follow the example of Christ.*

SUMMARY

Everything that happens in your life as a believer is designed to conform you into the image of Jesus Christ.

three

HOW TO RESPOND TO TRIALS

*I*t is both normal and natural to feel emotional pain when difficult times come into your life. But do not lose sight of why these painful moments occur; God, Who created the universe, so loves you that He is personally working in your life to conform you into His image. There can be no greater privilege or experience.

God has given us clear direction on how to respond when life's circumstances are unpleasant. Here are six things the Bible says to do when trials (big or small) come into your life.

1. DO NOT BE SURPRISED

Many Christians are blindsided and surprised when pain and suffering are introduced into their lives through a trial. Some Christians believe and expect that they should be spared such trouble and pain (big or small). Nothing could be further from the truth. We should not be surprised because Jesus told us clearly that tribulation (trouble) and life are inseparable:

> **JOHN 16:33**
> *These things I have spoken to you, that in Me you may have peace. In the world you will have tribulation; but be of good cheer, I have overcome the world.*

Peter also tells us that it is not strange or odd when trials come rushing into our life uninvited.

> **1 PETER 4:12**
> *Beloved, do not think it strange concerning the fiery trial which is to try you, as though some strange thing happened to you.*

Christians should never be surprised when they are insulted, made fun of, disrespected, or treated poorly by others. Peter tells us when an intense (burning) trial or serious trouble comes rushing suddenly into our life, view it as not only normal but expected. Peter then tells us that the trial is to "try us," that is, to refine our faith and to conform us into the image of His Son.

2. HAVE "CALM DELIGHT"

According to scholars, the book of James was written somewhere between 45 and 50 A.D. That makes James the first book written in the New Testament collection. Since this was the first book written, it carries with it great significance because the first written message delivered to Christians from God was how to understand and handle trials.

James is writing to Christian Jews that were scattered abroad (James 1:1) to exhort the early believers to maturity. In order to become mature they needed to understand why they were going through trials and difficulties and what to do. Here is how James began his instructions about trials:

JAMES 1:2
My brethren, count it all joy when you fall into various trials...

James starts by telling the Christians that it is a joyous occasion to be experiencing trials! What? Why would he say that? That's encouragement? Is James saying that we should throw a block party and do cart wheels in the streets when we are experiencing difficulties? Is James saying to not express sadness and act as if nothing is happening?

The answer lies in understanding the meaning of the word "joy" and the context of his encouragement. James is not saying that we should act as if nothing has happened, nor is he saying that we should hold it in and not express our feelings. The word "joy" means *calm delight*. James is saying that there should be a calm, peaceful feeling of delight because you know that God is at work in you and through the trial. We can be calmly delighted because the testing of our faith will result in maturity, James 1:4 states:

JAMES 1:4
But let patience have its perfect work, that you may be perfect and complete, lacking nothing

EVEN IN THE MIDST OF FIRE

Soon after I became a Christian, the Lord called me into the ministry. Like Jonah, I did not like what God was calling me to do, so I joined the Air Force instead. I was sent to Grand Forks, North Dakota.

A few years had passed when one evening while watching television I heard a popping noise coming from the back of our third floor apartment. I dismissed it until I heard it again a few minutes later. This time I went to the back of the apartment and discovered a fire had broken out and was rapidly spreading. We called the fire department and quickly left the apartment with only the clothes on our backs. It was twelve degrees outside. By the time the fire department arrived, the smoke was bellowing out of the windows. As I stood there watching everything we had going up in flames I thought, "The Lord is getting my attention." The calmness I felt was from the Lord knowing that He was working in my life and it was okay. The fire was later determined to have been started from faulty wiring in the floor. The popping noise I heard were light bulbs bursting because of the heat from the flames. The fire gutted only our third floor apartment.

It is significant that the first written message that God wanted Christians to hear was about enduring trials. It is also significant that the first thing God said about trials was to have calm delight when they occur. About twenty years after James said to have calm delight, the Apostle Peter said the same thing using a related word for joy.

1 PETER 4:13
But rejoice insofar as you share Christ's sufferings, that you may also rejoice and be glad when his glory is revealed.

The word "rejoice" here also means to be *calmly* happy. A proper response to what God is doing through fiery trials is to be calmly pleased that God is working to conform you into the image of His Son. Peter tells us to rejoice because we are sharing in the sufferings of Christ.

Paul wrote Colossians while he was in prison around 60 A.D. He had not been to the city but he was writing to encourage them in the faith and to speak about the false teaching to which they had been exposed. In his introduction, Paul prayed a magnificent prayer in which he asked that they would be strengthened with power so they would be patient through long-suffering *with joy* (Colossians 1:11). Paul prayed for them to endure through the tough times they were experiencing but do it with *joy.* It's the same word for joy that James and Peter uses that means *calm delight.* Paul is saying have calm delight because God is giving you the power to endure!

COLOSSIANS 1:9-14
For this reason we also, since the day we heard it, do not cease to pray for you, and to ask that you may be filled with the knowledge of His will in all wisdom and spiritual understanding; that you may walk worthy of the Lord, fully pleasing Him, being fruitful in every good work and increasing in the knowledge of God; strengthened with all might, according to His glorious power, for all patience and long-suffering with joy; giving thanks to the Father who has qualified us to be partakers of the inheritance of the saints in the light. He has delivered us from the power of darkness and conveyed us into the kingdom of the Son of His love, in whom we have redemption through His blood, the forgiveness of sins.

James, Peter and Paul used the same word for *joy* (calm delight) that Jesus used years earlier.

JOHN 15:11
These things I have spoken to you, that My joy may remain in you, and that your joy may be full.

Having *calm delight* during a trial or painful circumstance is the result of a proper understanding that God is working in your life.

3. ENDURE

The importance of enduring during a trial cannot be overstated. It is endurance that allows God to create in you Christ-like maturity. Don't pray for God to remove the trial, instead pray that He will give you patience to endure *in* the trial so you can learn of His Grace. James 1:3 states *"...knowing that the testing of your faith produces patience."*

The Greek word which is translated as "patience" is actually better translated as "endurance." A proper response to trials is *endurance* which means to *stay under*. The believer is to stay put in the trial and let God do His work.

Bible teacher and author Warren Wiersbe tells the story of being taught what farmers do while he was in grade school. He, like the other students, had been raised in the city and they were clueless as to what farmers did to grow crops. So the wise teacher gave each student a small flower pot, some dirt, and a seed to plant. She instructed that they were responsible to fill the flower pot with the dirt, plant the seed, give it water and sun every day. Warren said he was so curious as to how the seed was doing that he would dig it up every day! To no one's surprise, except Warren, the seed never grew. Warren said what he learned from that experience is to "bloom where you are planted." If you stay where you are (endure) you will grow toward maturity.

> **JAMES 1:4**
> *...but let endurance have its perfect work, that you may be perfect and complete, lacking nothing.*

James is saying that if you submit to your trial and see it as coming from God for your good, it will eventually make you a mature Christian. Do not run or hide from your trials, rather submit to the maturing process. If you fail to submit to what God is doing, you will remain immature. Dr. Tom Constable (Professor Emeritus, Dallas Theological Seminary) states in his notes on this passage...

> God will bring every believer who endures trials, rather than running from them, to maturity as we persevere in them. James taught that in view of this fact, we should rejoice in our trials rather than rebelling against them. They are God's instruments for perfecting us.

Talk about enduring trials; Paul penned the following words while he was in prison chained to a Roman soldier (CEV):

> **COLOSSIANS 4:2-6**
> *Never give up praying. And when you pray, keep alert and be thankful. Be sure to pray that God will make a way for us to spread his message and explain the mystery about Christ, even though I am in jail for doing this. Please pray that I will make the message as clear as possible. When you are with unbelievers, always make good use of the time. Be pleasant and hold their interest when you speak the message. Choose your words carefully and be ready to give answers to anyone who asks questions.*

Notice that Paul did not ask them to pray that he would be released from prison or that at least he would have the chains removed. Instead, he asked for prayer to make a way for the Gospel to be spread and to be made clear. Paul was not concerned about his circumstances. He viewed his circumstances as an opportunity to see God do His work in his trial. Paul was selfless and was more concerned for the guards and the believers at Colossae.

4. TRUST THE LORD

That's right, God wants you to trust Him no matter what is happening because He knows what He is doing.

> **PROVERBS 3:5-6**
> *Trust in the LORD with all your heart; and lean not on your own understanding. In all your ways acknowledge Him, and He shall direct your paths.*

Notice the contrast is between trusting the Lord and trusting your own understanding. If we trust the Lord, we cannot also depend upon our ability to understand what God is doing. We want to understand what is going on in our lives but many times we cannot make sense out of it. Sumner Wemp, my spiritual grandfather, said to me, that Proverbs 3:5-6 is teaching us not to try and figure it out. Just trust that the Lord knows what He is doing. Do not forget that it is God who is directing your life. It is God who determines what is best for you. It is God who has the final decision. Not you or I. It is God who sees the whole picture while we see only a tiny piece:

> To trust in the Lord with all our heart means we can't place our own right to understand above His right to direct our lives the way He sees fit. When we insist on God always making sense to our finite minds, we are setting ourselves up for spiritual trouble (author unknown).

My brother, Mike, author and pastor, wrote this comment on Proverbs 3:5-6:

> The Hebrew word for "direct" means "smooth, straight, right." Smooth is being free from obstacles. These verses are not promising daily direction in all the decisions we make. They are saying that if we follow the Lord, He will make our lives go straight in the sense of righteousness, smooth in the sense of removing all hindrances out of the way.

Solomon understood that God is working to produce in us His righteousness. His conclusion in this proverb is to trust the Lord and let Him do his work in you. It is a timeless truth.

> **PROVERBS 16:25**
> *There is a way that appears to be right, but in the end it leads to death.*

Our limited understanding can easily lead us down the wrong path. Just trust that the Lord knows what He is doing.

5. SEEK THE LORD

When trials come and we do not understand what He is doing, we are told to ask God for His wisdom.

> **JAMES 1:5**
> *If any of you lacks wisdom, let him ask of God, who gives to all liberally and without reproach, and it will be given to him.*

James is now showing us God's compassion. If you do not understand what God is doing in your circumstances, then ask God to give you His attitude toward what is happening. "Ask" is in the present tense so it actually means to keep on asking. Wisdom here is seeing life's circumstances from God's perspective--not yours.

This passage is encouraging us to keep asking God for His perspective until He opens our eyes. There is not a time reference in what James is saying; God may not immediately give you the answer you want.

...EVEN IF HE DOESN'T ANSWER RIGHT AWAY

I became the pastor of a small church of less than 40 people. Within a year we were drawing over 200 people with standing room only. God was blessing so we began looking for property to build a bigger facility. It suddenly came to light that one of the founding elders was involved in inappropriate and immoral behavior. I confronted him with the evidence and he resigned rather than face his accusers. It then became his mission to get me out of the church. I rallied everyone I knew to pray with me that this man would be stopped for the sake of the ministry. It did not work and I left. I was perplexed, "Why did God not answer my prayer and the prayers of godly people?" It stayed on my mind for the next seven years and I kept it before the Lord.

I was driving one day and once again seeking the Lord for an answer to my question, "Why didn't You answer my prayer?" After asking God the same question for seven years and hearing nothing, He finally answered! All of a sudden the Lord spoke clearly to me and said, "I did answer your prayer and the answer was no!"

Wow, I finally got it, His will was done! He allowed it to happen the way it did to fulfill His plan not mine. I was so relieved that I wept almost uncontrollably for ten minutes thanking the Lord for letting me know what I should have figured out. He did answer my prayer and the answer was no. When I understood, and after I finished weeping, I had calm delight come over me that I cannot put into words.

> **PSALM 3:36**
> *But You, O Lord, are a shield for me, My glory and the One who lifts up my head. I cried to the Lord with my voice, And He heard me from His holy hill. Selah. I lay down and slept; I awoke, for the Lord sustained me. I will not be afraid of ten thousands of people who have set themselves against me all around.*

...EVEN WHEN YOU'RE AFRAID

Many times in the Psalms, the writers cried out to the Lord for help in the middle of their trouble. Psalms 3 is a psalm of David written when his son Absalom was after him. Notice that David cried out to the Lord for help and God answered his prayer. David then had such peace that he was able to go to sleep! When he awoke he was no longer afraid. David sought the Lord even though he was extremely emotional and afraid.

As Christians we have the privilege of boldly asking God anything. The Contemporary English Version (CEV) captures the essence of this verse:

> **HEBREWS 4:16 (CEV)**
> *So whenever we are in need, we should come bravely before the throne of our merciful God. There we will be treated with undeserved kindness, and we will find help.*

6. REALIZE THAT GOD'S GRACE IS SUFFICIENT

God does not always answer your prayers the way you ask, nor does He always remove the situation from you. God is conforming you into the image of His Son by allowing things to come into your life, big and small. He may leave a thorn in your life to teach you that His Grace is sufficient. It's God's grace that sustains us in the trials that He brings into our lives. Notice the lesson that Paul learned from having a thorn in his life that God would not remove.

> **2 CORINTHIANS 12:7-10**
> *And lest I should be exalted above measure by the abundance of the*

> revelations, a thorn in the flesh was given to me, a messenger of Satan to buffet me, lest I be exalted above measure. Concerning this thing I pleaded with the Lord three times that it might depart from me. And He said to me, **"My grace is sufficient for you, for My strength is made perfect in weakness."** Therefore most gladly I will rather boast in my infirmities, that the power of Christ may rest upon me. Therefore I take pleasure in infirmities, in reproaches, in needs, in persecutions, in distresses, for Christ's sake. For when I am weak, then I am strong.

Paul realized that God was at work not by *removing* the thorn but by sustaining him *with* the thorn. Notice that when Paul understood that God was showing His grace and His power in his thorn he became glad! Paul understood that God's grace was sufficient to sustain him. Paul had boldly approached God but did not get the answer to his prayer that he wanted, instead he found something better--mercy and grace.

You may not understand how God is causing *"all things to work together for good"* (Romans 8:28) but when you trust Him with all your heart then you know that He is and you will discover that His grace is sufficient *in* the trial.

SUMMARY

Trials suddenly come into every Christian's life not unlike the 2014 huge mudslide in Washington state that caught everyone by surprise. Houses were swallowed up and cars driving by did not have time to avoid the avalanche of debris. Many lives were lost. No warning and no time to prepare.

Trials arrive unannounced and stay with us from a short moment to a long time and sometimes there is no end. Christians, however, do not have to be caught off guard when trials come because God has prepared us in His Word. The Scripture has given us at least six things we can do in order to be prepared for disturbing events that rush into our lives: (1) do not be surprised, (2) have calm delight knowing God is working in you, (3) be patient and endure the trial, (4) trust the Lord, (5) seek the Lord, and (6) realize that if He does not remove the trial that His grace is sufficient to sustain you in the trial.

four

INCORRECT RESPONSES TO TRIALS

When you respond *incorrectly* to trials by not accepting that God is at work conforming you into His image, you are likely to get anxious, angry, or depressed.

ANXIETY

When you remove the possibility that God is working in your circumstances, you will naturally become concerned about the outcome of what is happening. You then worry excessively that it may not turn out the way you would like. If your circumstances do not improve, your anxiety will turn into anger. This is the stage where other people or God are blamed for what is happening. Anger will eventually turn into depression where hope is lost that a favorable outcome will happen.

When you are being anxious, you shut the door on allowing God to give you peace and open the door for a flood of negative thinking about your circumstances. When you fail to involve God in what is causing you anxious concern you will be distracted from what God is doing in your life. When you are anxious, you are not accepting the trial as being used by God to conform you into the image of His Son. Instead, you will be surprised and overwhelmed at what is happening and you forfeit the opportunity to experience God's grace and peace. All of this happens when you fail to involve God in your trial and get anxious.

When you get anxious it shuts the door to allowing God to work and opens the door to becoming angry and depressed. When you are distracted by anxiety, you question the goodness of God and conclude that life isn't fair or it just doesn't make sense. God does not want you to be anxious about anything because He is in control of everything. According to Ephesians 1:11 He works all things according to His will:

EPHESIANS 1:11
In Him also we have obtained an inheritance, being predestined according to the purpose of Him who works all things according to the counsel of His will.

HOW TO RESPOND TO ANXIETY

Opportunities to become anxious are easy to find when you are experiencing a trial. Any level of anxiety can paralyze or interfere with your life as you know. The question is what can be done when you are feeling anxious about what is happening in your life? The issue of not getting anxious is mentioned several times in the Bible but the most popular passage is Philippians 4:6-7 which reads:

> *Be anxious for nothing, but in everything by prayer and supplication, with thanksgiving, let your requests be made known to God; and the peace of God, which surpasses all understanding, will guard your hearts and minds through Christ Jesus.*

Let's unpack this most important passage and discover the truth that God wants us all to practice. The Greek word in Philippians 4:6 that has been translated as "anxious" can also be translated to "care." *According to Vine's Expository Dictionary of New Testament Words*, care means "to draw in different directions, distract, hence signifies that which causes this, a care, especially an anxious care." The word "anxious" then holds the idea *to be drawn away by caring too much* which causes a distraction. Paul is not saying to not care, he is saying do not care to the point that you are anxious; do not have an *anxious* care. To be anxious is to be distracted, or better, when you are distracted, you become anxious. Distracted from what? **You are distracted from involving God in what is concerning you.**

NOTHING MEANS NOTHING

The word for *"nothing"* means *not one whit*. So nothing literally means nothing. When you take everything away from something, you are left with nothing. Paul is saying there is nothing for you be anxious or care about. Notice the contrast between being anxious for nothing and praying for everything. Two completely opposite extremes. Nothing means nothing and everything means everything. There is nothing over which I am to be anxious and I am not to overlook anything for which I am to pray. Now, the tense of this Greek word "nothing" is prohibiting an action that is already underway. So Paul is saying to the Christians in Philippi, you are distracted because you are caring too much so stop it *right now!*

To not be anxious is a command, not a suggestion. Paul is saying STOP being anxious. Since it is a command, it is possible for you to choose to not be anxious. So, if you want to get beyond being anxious about anything, then make the choice to quote this verse the very moment you find yourself getting anxious and then make a choice not to be. Give the situation to God and let Him do as He wills. God will grant you peace because He honors His Word and He meets you at the point of your obedience. You become what you think about, so the more you think about not being anxious, the less anxious you will become.

GIVE THANKS

Notice that the phrase *"be anxious for nothing"* in verse 4 is immediately followed by Paul telling us to pray. So when you pray, you are involving God in what is going *on* that is causing you anxious care. Notice also that your prayer is to include thanksgiving. That means that you pray thanking God for the outcome-- whatever it is, whether it's to your liking or not! Leave the outcome to God because He knows what is best for you.

RECEIVE PEACE

As you read on in the verse, you find that when you pray with thanksgiving, God will give you peace to guard both your emotions (heart) and mind! Guard you from what? You will be guarded from being anxious! And Paul adds that the peace is so terrific that it will exceed anything you could understand or imagine! Actually, you can't explain what's it's like, it has to be experienced.

It is a command to not be anxious and when we obey and ask God for help, He gives us peace and protection. The peace is so great that it protects our emotions and mind from becoming anxious. If you want God's peace, involve Him in what you are going through by praying with thanksgiving. Praying with thanksgiving means being willing to accept whatever He does.

The following illustration is over a small incident, but it illustrates the point. My wife said to me one day that she wanted a pergola. Not knowing what she meant I reasoned that it had something to do with brewing coffee and responded with a puzzled look. She used another word and said, "It's like an Arbor" and I understood. We came up with a rough design and built the pergola over the next few months. After it was finished, we received a notice from the home owners association that it was in violation of the rules. Yikes, I had not thought about asking permission before we built. We decided immediately that we were not going to be anxious about the outcome of their investigation. I supplied all the information they requested and waited for their decision. We both maintained that we were not going to be anxious, even if we had to tear it down. Weeks went by and on a Sunday morning while waiting for the church service to start, my thoughts drifted to the fate of the pergola. Lots of time, money and hard work went into the construction of the magnificent structure, but I said to the Lord, "Whatever You decided is okay. If it needs to come down then we'll take it down." At that very moment I was flooded with the peace that passes all understanding. It was so wonderful that I could no longer pray about the fate of the pergola. It just didn't matter, I was at peace. After the service and as we were walking out I shared the experience with my wife and she said, "Wow, the exact same thing happened to me!" We compared the times and it happened to both of us at the very same moment. As it turned out they let us keep it with slight modification.

This was a small and insignificant event, however it could have been an opportunity to be anxious and not trust the Lord. We both decided to not be anxious and to accept whatever God wanted. If you choose to not be anxious with the small things that happen, you will be able to do the same when the big events rush into your life. Philippians 4:6-7 is so key to growing spiritually that it's importance cannot be overstated. The anxiety battle must be won to prevent missing what God has for you. Be prepared, practice Philippians 4:6-7 daily.

Jesus reiterates this call for us to not be drawn away or distracted by caring too much about what we are going to eat, drink, wear or what will happen tomorrow.

MATTHEW 6:31-34
Therefore do not worry, saying, 'What shall we eat?' or 'What shall we drink?' or 'What shall we wear?' For after all these things the Gentiles seek. For your heavenly Father knows that you need all these things. But seek first the kingdom of God and His righteousness, and all these things shall be added to you. Therefore do not worry about tomorrow, for tomorrow will worry about its own things. Sufficient for the day is its own trouble.

The scripture is clear, Christian's are never to be anxious about anything at anytime.

ANGER

If you allow anxiety to linger in your thoughts, it could easily develop into anger. You will view your circumstances as not being fair, right, or as punishment from God. You will not see God's goodness and grace in your circumstances and become angry toward Him or the people involved. I commonly hear, "I do not understand what God is doing to me!" and "Why do these things always happen to me?"

Both statements reflect anger.

The couple that lost one of their twin daughters to drowning were still angry five years after the event. I listened to them talk for an hour and a half about their life. It was obvious that they were exceedingly angry at God for allowing their daughter to drown. I pointed out to them that they were angry at God and the emotional explosion that happened next was shocking! The 6' 4" husband immediately stood to his feet, leaned over the table and shook his finger in my face screaming that they were not angry at God! It was clear that neither of them were able to seek God's grace in what had happened. The mother of the child was feeling guilty for not giving more attention to what her daughter was doing. The father was angry at his wife for neglecting her most important duty of protecting the children. They both blamed God for allowing the incident to happen.

Losing a child is the most difficult thing to deal with in life. I can't explain it nor did I try with this couple. Our responsibility, even in a tragedy like this, is to allow God to do His work in our heart and learn that His grace is sufficient.

HOW TO HANDLE ANGER

Anger is not an option. James, the half-brother of Christ, wrote a letter to encourage the Jews that had been dispersed. They were having trials and James wanted them to understand why, what to do, and what not to do.

In chapter one, James explains the purpose of trials and gives guidance as how to respond and how not to respond. James is saying that the reason for trials is to produce maturity (Christ-likeness). So be patient and let the trial do its work. James warns them not to be angry over what is happening in verses 19-20: *"So then, my beloved brethren, let every man be swift to hear, slow to speak, slow to wrath; for the wrath of man does not produce the righteousness of God."*

If you get angry about the difficulties you experience, you will miss the righteousness of God that is being taught in the trial. We are to receive the Word with meekness:

JAMES 1:21
Therefore lay aside all filthiness and overflow of wickedness, and receive with meekness the implanted word, which is able to save your souls.

Not all anger is sin. Righteous indignation is a form of anger that is not considered sin. It is an emotional reaction over a sense of injustice, like the mistreatment of another person. Jesus, for example, drove the money lenders out of the temple (Matthew 21:12-13). All other anger is sin and is not allowed within a Christian. Consider the following passages:

ECCLESIASTES 7:9
Do not be quickly provoked in your spirit, for anger resides in the lap of fools.

PROVERBS 14:29
A patient man has great understanding, but a quick-tempered man displays folly.

PROVERBS 15:1
A gentle answer turns away wrath, but a harsh word stirs up anger.

PROVERBS 15:18
A hot-tempered person stirs up conflict, but the one who is patient calms a quarrel.

PROVERBS 16:32
Better a patient man than a warrior, a man who controls his temper than one who takes a city.

PROVERBS 29:11
A fool gives full vent to his anger, but a wise man keeps himself under control.

1 CORINTHIANS 13:5
Love is not provoked.

EPHESIANS 4:2
Be ye angry and sin not, let not the sun go down on your wrath.

COLOSSIANS 3:8
But now you must rid yourselves of all such things as these: anger, rage, malice, slander, and filthy language from your lips.

God says if you do get angry, deal with it quickly. Anger harms relationships and prevents God from doing His work in your heart. God calls an angry person a fool because of their blindness to the impact their anger has on others (Ecclesiastes 7:9). Believers are to walk in love and love does not get provoked (1 Corinthians 13:5).

DEPRESSION

If your response to life's difficulties is anxiety and anger, it will eventually turn into depression. Depression is a feeling of sadness and dejection that alters a person's emotional and mental state and interferes with their daily life functions in varying degrees. Symptoms range from mild to severe and can be short term or last for an extended period of time.

Before I go further, please understand that some down feelings are not only appropriate but normal and expected. For example, if you were to lose a loved one through death, you would be expected to feel deep emotions and have normal activities like eating, sleeping and working interrupted. After a period of time has elapsed, these functions return to normal and we continue our journey through this life. Sometimes changes in mood are related to hormonal changes like those experienced by women. For the most part, however, those who report they are "depressed" are focused on one or more problems. Life has overwhelmed them, a tragic event has happened, something did not happen as expected, someone did something to them or they did something to someone else...the list is endless.

It is different, however, when a Christian routinely gets depressed over the painful events in their life. It is different when a Christian retreats and withdraws from life to pout or fume about their circumstances. It is different when a Christian reacts negatively to events, gets angry, and depressed.

DEPRESSION AS A ROUTINE RESPONSE

When depression is a routine response to the difficulties in life, people are living examples of what the stoic philosopher Epictetus (A.D. c. 55–135) said 2,000 years ago: *"People are disturbed, not by things or events, but by the views (perceptions) which they take of them."* What disturbs you is not what happens but what you **think** about what happens. It's not the event, it's what you **think** about the event-- it's your perception.

People who get depressed disturb themselves by rehearsing their negative thoughts (perceptions) of the event. Depressed people therefore, *think too much about the wrong thing.* People who are depressed are *not* trying to *solve* the problem, they are embedded *in* the problem by reviewing the negatives and fuming over the wrongness of the event. People who are depressed are therefore *choosing* to be miserable.

To prevent being miserable and getting depressed, do not rehearse negative thoughts about your circumstances. Choose to see that your circumstances are designed by God to conform you into the image of His Son (Romans 8:28-29).

JONAH'S EXAMPLE

Christians that get depressed are stuck **in** and focused **on**, the problem. Christians who get depressed, fail to see--or do not accept--what God is doing in their lives through their circumstances. Jonah is an example of what happens when you don't accept what God is doing in your life.

In Jonah 1:1-4,11, the Lord told Jonah to go to Nineveh and preach repentance. Jonah did not think that was such a good idea because the Ninevites were enemies of Israel and he wanted to see them destroyed, not spared. So he bought a ticket on a boat going in the opposite direction, which seemed like a good idea at the time. The Lord then sent a storm (Jonah 1:4) to get Jonah's attention. (May I pause to say that this is exactly the purpose of any storm that moves into our life...God is trying to get our attention.) Well the crew eventually figured out that the problem was Jonah (Jonah 1:7) and he was thrown overboard (Jonah 1:15). We know what happened next, a rather large fish swallowed Jonah. This was another attention getting maneuver and it worked.

Jonah prayed (Jonah 2:1)! God answered his prayer and the fish spit Jonah out onto dry land. With his new enlightenment, Jonah headed for Nineveh and delivered the message God had given him (Jonah 3:4). Jonah's message from God was received and the city repented (Jonah 3:5-10). Again, Jonah reacted with rebellion and anger toward God at what He was doing (Jonah 4:1) and then he became depressed (Jonah 4:8-9). When God did not do what Jonah wanted Him to do he got angry, depressed, and wanted to die. Blinded by these emotions, Jonah could not see that God was doing something not only for Nineveh but for him. God demonstrated His Grace to Nineveh and Jonah missed the lesson.

These emotions expressed by Jonah are not uncommon among Christians that are displeased or confused about what God is doing in their life. We are not to be dismayed according to Deuteronomy 31:8: *"It is the LORD who goes before you. He will be with you; he will not leave you or forsake you. Do not fear or be dismayed."*

The Hebrew word for "dismayed" means to break down either (literally) by violence, or (figuratively) by confusion and fear, hence to be discouraged or to be terrified. The message is clear. We are not to be discouraged or terrified because God will not leave you or forsake you! David learned this lesson.

PSALM 40:1-3
...I waited patiently for the LORD; he inclined to me and heard my cry. He drew me up from the pit of destruction, out of the miry bog, and set my feet upon a rock, making my steps secure. He put a new song in my

mouth, a song of praise to our God. Many will see and fear, and put their trust in the LORD.

THERE ARE NO HAPPY DEPRESSED PEOPLE

In all my years as a therapist, I have never known a happy depressed person. People that come to me with the symptoms of depression are dealing with a disappointing life event and they are stuck. I have also never dealt with anyone that reported symptoms of depression who was unable to identify an event that was causing their emotional pain.

Depressed people do not think about positive things, they think about that which is negative. Remember, depression occurs when you *think too much about the wrong thing*. Instead of thinking that life's circumstances are coming from God for their good, depressed people believe that life is unfair or that God is punishing them. They are thinking about the wrong thing and that leads to depression and/or anger toward God.

Christians open the door to depression when they fail to obey Philippians 4:6-7, become anxious about their concern, and do not involve God by praying. Depressed Christians do not take God's view about their concern. As soon as you accept that God is at work and you see the circumstance from His point of view, you will no longer be depressed. When you fail to recognize and involve the Lord in your life you forfeit peace, growth, and His blessings.

Paul had more to say following his direction to not be anxious in Philippians 4:6-7. The next verse (v.8) identifies what we should be thinking about:

PHILIPPIANS 4:8
Finally, brethren, whatever things are true, whatever things are noble, whatever things are just, whatever things are pure, whatever things are lovely, whatever things are of good report, if there is any virtue and if there is anything praiseworthy—meditate on these things.

Paul gives us a list of positive virtues that should occupy our thoughts. Translated, the word "meditate" carries with it the idea of *careful reflection* (cf. Psalms 1). Paul is saying to carefully reflect on things that are wholesome and healthy. When you do, you will experience the peace of God:

PHILIPPIANS 4:9
The things which you learned and received and heard and saw in me, these do, and the God of peace will be with you.

A REMARKABLE REVERSAL

I worked at a mental hospital for several years in Dallas, Texas. I was routinely called to evaluate people that were at one of eleven hospital emergency rooms in Dallas County.

At 2 A.M. I was called to evaluate a young man to see if he needed to be committed to our facility for treatment. The ER doctor told me that the young man's wife had left him and was living in a crack house, addicted to cocaine. He had tried everything to get her back, but had failed. He stopped eating and was severely depressed. He was actually starving himself to death over his grief and love for his wife. Out of desperation his sister took him the hospital. She told me that he and his wife were both Christians.

At first he would not look at me, he just sat there with his head down. I explained to him that God cared more about her than he did and that this was God's problem to solve, not his. He had exhausted all of his efforts and now it was time to let God take over. I encouraged him to let God take care of his wayward wife and for him to trust God in what seemed to be an impossible situation. He did not respond. I turned my attention to his sister and after a few minutes had passed, I looked over and he was standing. His countenance was remarkably different. He said, "This is not my problem, it is God's problem!" Turning his attention to his sister he then said, "I'm hungry, let's go get something to eat!" This young man made a remarkable reversal of his emotional state when he made the decision to let God solve his problem.

HOW SCRIPTURE TACKLES DEPRESSION

The Bible was written over a sixteen hundred year period and from the beginning God had something to say about being depressed.

> **DEUTERONOMY 31:8**
> … *It is the LORD who goes before you. He will be with you; he will not leave you or forsake you. Do not fear or be dismayed.*

The Hebrew word translated "leave" has the idea of *leave alone*. The word that immediately follows is "forsake" which means *to leave destitute or fail*. The Hebrew word translated "dismayed" means to *break down*, either (literally) by violence, or (figuratively) *by confusion and fear; to beat down, cause to be discouraged.* So Moses, the writer of Deuteronomy, has given us three reasons to not be discouraged or depressed. First, God goes before you which means He holds the future and He is leading you. Second, He is with you which means He is beside you. Thirdly, He will never fail you or leave you destitute.

With promises like this there is no reason to ever be discouraged or depressed. God is there for you and always will be. God continued to encourage us throughout the Bible to wait on Him, to hope in Him, and to humble ourselves before Him as noted in the following verses:

PSALMS 40:1-3
I waited patiently for the LORD; he inclined to me and heard my cry. He drew me up from the pit of destruction, out of the miry bog, and set my feet upon a rock, making my steps secure. He put a new song in my mouth, a song of praise to our God. Many will see and fear, and put their trust in the LORD.

PSALMS 42:11
Why are you cast down, O my soul, and why are you in turmoil within me? Hope in God; for I shall again praise him, my salvation and my God.

1 PETER 5:6-7
Humble yourselves therefore under the mighty hand of God, that he may exalt you in due time: Casting all your care upon him; for he careth for you.

SUMMARY

When trials come into your life and you do not accept the circumstances as coming from God, you open the door to becoming anxious about what is happening. Anxiety leads to anger and anger leads to depression.

Once you become anxious over something, you remove God from involvement in what is causing you to be anxious. You are then distracted from God's purpose for the event...conforming you into the image of His Son (Romans 8:28-29).

When you do not accept that God is conforming you into the image of His Son, you will be distracted from what God is doing in your life. You will not be patient, nor will you trust the Lord. You will then forfeit peace and will not grow spiritually. By accepting that God is at work in your life through your circumstances, you allow God to do His work in creating His likeness in you.

five

CONSEQUENCES OF INCORRECT RESPONSES TO TRIALS

We have been given specific instructions on how to handle trials when they rush into our lives. When we respond incorrectly to trials we often get anxious, angry, and depressed. These emotions will be temporary if you embrace what God is doing in your life and allow Him to use your circumstances to be part of conforming you into His own image. The consequences of incorrectly responding to trials you experience are clearly spelled out in Scripture. The book of James is so important in understanding trials that once again we turn to it for insight. It is here that we find two consequences to not responding correctly to trials. A third consequence is found in Hebrews 12:11-15.

YOU WILL NOT GROW SPIRITUALLY

In the following passage, James makes it clear that in order to grow spiritually you must be patient during the trial.

> **JAMES 1:3-4**
> ...knowing that the testing of your faith produces patience. But let patience have its perfect work, that you may be perfect [mature] and complete, lacking nothing.

By being patient you will be allowing God to use your life's experiences to move you along toward maturity.

Being patient also means you don't get anxious when life takes a sudden, painful turn. Being patient means you do not get frustrated and angry, nor do you blame God or someone else when something does not turn out the way you wanted. Being patient means you do not lose hope and get depressed because you can see the benefit of the trial. Being patient means that you trust that God knows what He is doing and that it is best for you.

If you are not patient during a trial, you will not grow into maturity and you will experience anxiety, and perhaps anger and depression when the next trial occurs.

YOU WILL BE UNSTABLE

James recognizes that trials can be overwhelming and confusing so he encourages his readers to ask God if they need the wisdom to understand the difficulty.

> **JAMES 1:5-8**
> *If any of you lacks wisdom, let him ask of God, who gives to all liberally and without reproach, and it will be given to him. But let him ask in faith, with no doubting, for he who doubts is like a wave of the sea driven and tossed by the wind. For let not that man suppose that he will receive anything from the Lord; he is a double-minded man, unstable in all his ways.*

The word translated "double-minded" is used only in the book of James and appears twice: James 1:8 and James 4:8. According to Strong's Hebrew and Greek Dictionary the word means *two spirited, that is, vacillating (in opinion or purpose); double minded*. James is saying that if you vacillate about what God is doing because you do not see it as coming from Him for your good and yet you still ask God for help...you will not get it. Such a person is not sincere when they pray. This Christian might pray the right prayer asking God for help but their heart is not convinced that God is at work. Such a person vacillates between believing and not believing that God is working in the trial. Such a person is controlled, not by truth, but by their emotions which fluctuate during the trial.

The consequence of not responding to your trials appropriately is that you will flip-flop between opinions which means there will be an internal struggle. You trust then you don't trust, you believe and then you do not believe. When you are not trusting God, you become anxious over the outcome of the trial; will it turn out okay or not? There will be conflict between believing at times that God is at work and believing at other times that God is not in what is happening. You can trust and obey but only for a day and then you doubt God once again. A double-minded person has a divided allegiance and opinion and sends a confusing message to those who are around them.

James is saying that God wants us to take His view of trials. Namely, that He is at work in our trials and He wants us to endure in the difficulty so He can produce in us maturity. Knowing that God is at work is the reason we can have calm delight as we experience the trial. James gives us a warning that if we are inconsistent in trusting God in our trials, we will be double-minded, miss what God is teaching us, and remain immature.

YOU WILL HAVE A NEGATIVE IMPACT ON OTHERS

The consequences of not responding to trials correctly impacts not only you but also those in your sphere of influence, like your family and church community.

> ### HEBREWS 12:11-15
> *Now no chastening seems to be joyful for the present, but painful; nevertheless, afterward it yields the peaceable fruit of righteousness to those who have been trained by it. Therefore strengthen the hands which hang down, and the feeble knees, and make straight paths for your feet, so that what is lame may not be dislocated, but rather be healed. Pursue peace with all people, and holiness, without which no one will see the Lord: looking carefully lest anyone fall short of the grace of God; lest any root of bitterness springing up cause trouble, and by this many become defiled;*

Dr. Mike Cocoris comments in his unpublished notes on Hebrews 12:15:

> The idea of a root of bitterness is taken from Deuteronomy 29:18, where an idol worshiper, that is, an apostate is a root of bitterness among the people. Likewise, in the context of Hebrews an apostate can cause trouble and defile others within the congregation.

The end result of not accepting God's help in your trial will be that you negatively influence others. The word "defile" means to *taint* or *contaminate*. Your rejection of God's help in the trial gives others, who are also weak in the faith, permission to follow your example. This is teaching that the sin of one can influence an entire community of Christians.

SUMMARY

The Scripture identifies at least three consequences of responding incorrectly to trials. First, a believer will not grow to maturity (James 1:3-4). Second, a believer will be unstable in all his ways (James 1:8). Third, a believer will have a negative influence on those that observe their incorrect response (Hebrews 12:11-15). These three incorrect responses to the circumstances in life will produce not only an immature Christian but also a destructive one.

part two
RELATIONSHIPS

RELATIONSHIP STRUGGLES

Another reason Christians seek counseling is due to a deteriorating relationship. The counseling that I've done for decades has mostly centered around conflict between two people who are married. I've also been involved in pre-marital counseling and found that even before a couple married, problems were already being manifested.

By the time a married couple seeks help, the relationship has significantly deteriorated to the point that many have more of a partnership than a marriage. Some issues between people begin as petty disagreements but grow into larger issues that sometimes lead to divorce. To understand why we have problems in relationships, we need to start at the beginning of the human race.

ADAM'S SIN

God created Adam and gave him the job of keeping the garden (Genesis 2:15), *"Then the Lord God took the man and put him in the garden of Eden to tend and keep it."* Then God told him to not eat of a specific tree in the garden:

GENESIS 2:16-17
And the Lord God commanded the man, saying, "Of every tree of the garden you may freely eat; but of the tree of the knowledge of good and evil you shall not eat, for in the day that you eat of it you shall surely die.

Adam was told clearly and directly what to do and what not to do. God even told him what the consequences would be if he disobeyed--he would die.

God then gave to Adam his wife. Now there are two people alone on the planet and they were both sinless. The command is not repeated in the Scripture to not eat of that tree because God held Adam responsible to obey and to get his wife to obey. As we know, that is not what happened.

Chapter 3 opens with a revelation that there is evil in the garden in the form of a serpent. Adam's wife has a conversation with the evil serpent which proved to be their downfall. The serpent asked if indeed she would die if she ate of the fruit of that forbidden tree. She was persuaded and desired to be wise so she made a choice and took a bite out of the fruit. If that was all that had happened, sin would not have entered the human race but that was not the end of the story.

The passage does not suggest that Adam was far away and unaware of what was happening. Adam was apparently close enough to hear their conversation and did nothing to stop the woman from disobeying God's clear and direct command. The woman did not have to call for Adam to come closer, she just handed the once bitten fruit to him. He took the fruit without question or protest and made a choice to disobey God's command and ate. It was then that something happened. With one bite, innocence was lost and their eyes were immediately opened, they saw that they were naked and were ashamed. The evil serpent's mission had been accomplished, Adam and the woman were now sinners because they had rebelled against God's authority and did not follow His instructions.

THE RESULTS OF ADAM'S SIN

THREE SEPARATIONS

Adam's sin caused three separations. First, it caused Adam to be separated from God. Adam no longer had the same relationship with God after he sinned that he had before he sinned. Second, Adam's sin separated him from the woman. Remember, Adam immediately blamed God and the woman (later named Eve) for his choice. Imagine how she must have felt! Third, Adam's sin separated him from himself. His sin blinded him so quickly that he would not admit his wrong choice and rationalized that it wasn't his fault.

THE HEART WAS AFFECTED

The effect of sin is immediately seen in Adam and the woman's attitude toward God. All three aspects of the heart (mind, emotion, and will) were now in opposition toward God. They chose to rebel (will), they were afraid of God (emotion) and they rationalized away their responsibility (mind) to God.

Notice how Adam and the woman responded to God's questions in Genesis 3:8-13. God asked, *"Adam, where are you?"* Adam responded, *"I heard Your voice in the garden and I was afraid because I was naked, and I hid myself."* God had more questions (Genesis 3:11), *"Who told you that you were naked? Have you eaten from the tree of which I commanded you that you should not eat?"* Again, God knew the answers. He was giving Adam a second chance to confess but once again he failed to own his disobedience. Adam responded (Genesis 3:12), *"The woman whom You gave to be with me, she gave me of the tree, and I ate."* He wasn't getting anywhere with Adam so God now turns to the woman with a question (Genesis 3:13), *"What is this you have done?"* The woman said, *"The serpent deceived me, and I ate."*

Adam and the woman were factual in their response but they rationalized the reason for their choices. Adam actually accused God of causing him to disobey: *"The woman whom YOU gave to be with me, SHE gave me fruit from the tree, and I ate"* (Genesis 3:12 emphasis mine). Adam now viewed God's good gift to him (the woman) as the source of his trouble which shows how far he fell so quickly.

JEREMIAH 17:9
The heart is deceitful above all things, and desperately wicked; who can know it?

This passage is not teaching us that a person can deceive another, it is teaching that every person is capable of self-deception. The Adamic nature that we all possess is so blinding that we easily deceive ourselves into believing something is true when it is not. Dr. Tom Constable, (Professor, Emeritus Bible Exposition, Dallas Theological Seminary) captures the essence of this passage in his notes on Jeremiah:

> The human heart is deceptive; we may think we know why we do something, but really we may be doing it for another reason. It is naturally incurably sick, really totally depraved, and in need of healing. No one really understands his or her own corrupt heart, nor do we understand why our hearts behave as they do.

Jesus removes all doubt as to the real problem we all have! This is not only a diagnosis, it's an indictment! Look no further to identify our problem than the sinful heart:

MATTHEW 15:18-20
But those things which proceed out of the mouth come from the heart, and they defile a man. For out of the heart proceed evil thoughts, murders, adulteries, fornications, thefts, false witness, blasphemies. These are the things which defile a man, but to eat with unwashed hands does not defile a man.

BEHAVIOR HAS NOT CHANGED

Adam and Eve's actions in the Garden of Eden unfortunately still reflects our actions today. They disobeyed God's command, became defensive when confronted, failed to take responsibility, rationalized their choices, and tried to justify their behavior by shifting the blame. More than six thousand years have passed and billions of people have been born and nothing has changed; we are still rebelling against God's authority and failing to take responsibility for our behavior. We still get defensive when confronted with our rebellious choices, we still fail to take personal responsibility, and we still rationalize and blame someone or something else for our behavior.

Is it any wonder that we have problems today? It isn't a mystery when two people come together to live happily ever after and they don't! Then add children! Several children. So much for harmony and peace! It's easy to see that we need some serious help!

RELATIONSHIPS DETERIORATE SLOWLY

People grow apart because of how they treat each other. Sounds obvious but couples do not accept responsibility for how they treat each other and as a result the relationship slowly slips away. They argue and blame each other and by the time they seek help, destructive patterns have become deeply embedded in how they relate to each other. The conflict goes on for so long that one or both simply give up trying.

You may be reading this because your relationship is moving in the wrong direction. The good news is the direction of your relationship can be reversed if you are willing to make some changes in how you communicate.

A relationship will deteriorate slowly over the years when two people disagree with each other, argue, and get angry. It is usually over spending money, sex, relatives, raising the children, unfinished projects around the home, not spending time with each other, where to set the thermostat, etc. You get the idea. People disagree and argue their point trying to be right and win. The issue is usually not resolved and both walk away feeling annoyed, angry, hurt, and resentful.

When the disagreement is not resolved peacefully, a little residue is left over like a small amount of dust on furniture. At first you can't notice it but over time as more and more dust accumulates, it becomes obvious to everyone. The residue left over from an argument and getting angry leaves a bitter taste in your mouth. You are left with feelings of resentment. Each one has a little resentment because of what was said and how it was said during the argument. Apologies may be exchanged but still the residue is there. The residue collects over time and that feeling of resentment turns into bitterness toward each other.

As resentment accumulates over the years, each person builds a wall around themselves for protection. Every argument is noted and the details are chiseled in a brick and carefully placed in the wall. Brick by brick the wall is built. Higher and higher. Wider and wider. The years pass and one day you wake up and you've hit the proverbial wall. You think the relationship is over. You have nothing more to say. You are not being heard by your spouse and you've decided it is a waste of time to try and communicate.

WHERE DO YOU SIT ON THE COUCH?

I have noticed over the years that when I do pre-marital counseling, the soon-to-be-married love birds sit close to each other on the couch, they touch and hold hands. But when married couples are having problems and come in for counseling they do not sit close to each other on the couch. Really, the further apart they sit from each other on the couch, the more damage there is in the relationship. Sometimes there is enough room between them for four more people! The distance between them represents the severity of the damage in the relationship.

HOW TO RESTORE A DAMAGED RELATIONSHIP

There is no hope for dealing with life's difficulties apart from knowing, understanding, and doing what God has told us to do. Not doing what God said got us into this mess--Adam's sin. Doing what God said will get us out of the mess we're in. The emphasis here is on *doing*. Charles Swindoll, evangelical Christian pastor said, "Wisdom occurs when knowledge produces obedience." It is not just about *knowing* what God said, it is about *doing* what God said.

Adam and Eve did not believe that what God had told them was best for them so they did it their way. We do the same thing today. Most do not believe that the instructions God recorded in His Word are best for us, so we try to do it our way--without success.

DO WHAT GOD SAID

The choice every Christian must make is whether or not he or she will do what God has said. The Bible is our manual for living, however just *knowing* the Bible is not enough. It is possible to know all the right things, to have wisdom and insight, teach others, and yet still follow a course of extreme foolishness and rebellion.

In James 1:22, James is very clear that knowing is not only not enough, he goes so far as to say if you *just* know the Word you are deceived: *"But be doers of the word, and not hearers only, deceiving yourselves."* The deception comes from only hearing the Word but not doing what the Word says. We must actually do what God says.

DRAW A CIRCLE

Is there any hope of restoring a damaged relationship? Can it be put back together? Can it be good again?

The answer is yes, *if* you are willing to accept responsibility for your part in the demise of the relationship. Draw two imaginary circles. Now imagine that you are in one and your spouse is in the other. The first and most important step in restoring a damaged relationship is to deal *only* with what's in your circle--you. You cannot fix another person so don't try. You can only fix you and if you do that then you are halfway to recovering the damaged relationship. Your mate must choose to work only on his or her circle--not yours.

You are responsible for the wall that you built. Building the wall between you and your mate was your choice. You built it and you can tear it down. You could have responded another way but you chose to erect the wall between you and your mate. I know, your mate is responsible too, but we're dealing with your circle.

Warren Wiersbe, author and Bible Conference speaker said, **"The heart of every problem is the problem of the heart."** Whether or not change can occur depends on the person's heart attitude and response to God's Word. The Scripture is clear, the only people who can be helped are those with an open heart and who are seeking God's wisdom to apply to their life. Those with a heart of pride refuse to accept direction or correction.

> **PROVERBS 1:7**
> *The fear of the LORD is the beginning of knowledge, but fools despise wisdom and instruction.*

SUMMARY

We all have a rebellious heart that we inherited from Adam. We do not want to be accountable for our behavior so we get defensive, rationalize, and shift blame to someone or something else. Living the Spiritual life is about being conformed into His image so we will be like Him and not do these things. The responsibility of every Christian is to know what God said and apply it to our lives every day.

seven

TREAT OTHERS THE WAY GOD TREATS YOU

How we are to treat each other is clearly identified in Scripture. When we fail to do as God says, relationships are damaged and sometimes destroyed.

I counseled a couple that had been married for ten years and had two small children. They had a disagreement over something so insignificant that if you knew what it was, you would laugh out loud...really. The husband had to move out of their home because of his wife's emotional explosion. After a few sessions with him, his wife agreed to come for a counseling session. They sat on the couch-- she sat all the way to the left and he sat all the way to the right.

He was willing to do whatever it took to restore the damaged relationship but she was not. She was angry at him and refused to forgive him for an incident that did not need forgiveness. Nevertheless, she was angry and she needed to forgive him for her sake. After a few hours I asked her this question, "Do you want God to treat you the way you treat other people?" I motioned toward her husband. She did not look at him but answered quickly, "No!" I then said, "Okay, then treat other people the same way God treats you." She refused and within a few months, the marriage ended in divorce.

If all couples treated each other the way God treats them there would not be a need for interventions. We have problems in relationships because we do not do what God tells us to do. If you are having trouble in your marriage or in another relationship ask yourself, "Am I treating that person the way God treats me?" If the answer is no, then remain in your circle and begin today doing the following three things (this is how God treats you):

1. LOVE UNCONDITIONALLY

The Bible is clear about God's love. He loves you unconditionally and nothing can separate you from His love. It is because of God's great love for you that you were brought to salvation.

JOHN 3:16
For God so loved the world that He gave His only begotten Son, that whoever believes in Him should not perish but have everlasting life.

ROMANS 5:8
But God demonstrates His own love toward us, in that while we were still sinners, Christ died for us.

ROMANS 8:38-39
For I am persuaded that neither death nor life, nor angels nor principalities nor powers, nor things present nor things to come, nor height nor depth, nor any other created thing, shall be able to separate us from the love of God which is in Christ Jesus our Lord.

JOHN 13:34-35
A new commandment I give to you, that you love one another; as I have loved you, that you also love one another. By this all will know that you are My disciples, if you have love for one another.

1 JOHN 4:11
Beloved, if God so loved us, we also ought to love one another.

Because God demonstrated His love toward us, we are to demonstrate the same kind of love to others. God loves us without conditions, regardless of what we do. This is the way you are to love your mate and the other important people in your life. Jesus made it clear that we are to love others because He first loved us.

HOW UNCONDITIONAL LOVE BEHAVES

1 Corinthians 13:4-8 is known as the love chapter because it clearly identifies just how love acts. The Greek word used for love in 1 Corinthians 13:4-8 is *agape*. It seeks the highest good for someone. It is unconditional and refers to love that God is (1 John 4:8,16), that God shows (John 3:16, 1 John 4:9) and that God enables in His children (Galatians 5:22-23).

Agape chooses self-sacrifice to serve the one being loved. It is the highest form of love and it is volitional and not selective. Agape is not based on pleasant emotions or good feelings, it is the love from the will (a conscious choice) and not motivated by appearance or emotions. If two people loved each other this way, there would be no arguments and no demise in the relationship. This passage tells us just how *agape* behaves toward others:

1 CORINTHIANS 13:4-8

VERSE 4:
1. *Love is **patient***: Love never takes the opportunity to avenge itself.
2. *Love is **kind***: Love never offends, insults or says anything unkind.
3. *Love is **not jealous***: Love does not desire what another person has in an evil way.
4. *Love **does not brag***: Love does not draw attention to itself.
5. *Love is **not puffed up***: Love does not have a superior attitude.

VERSE 5:
6. *Love is **not rude***: Love has good manners and you makes you feel comfortable.
7. *Love **seeks not its own***: Love does not trade being right for another person's feelings.
8. *Love is **not provoked***: Love does not get irritated.
9. *Love **thinks no evil***: Love does not keep an account of evil deeds, it forgives.

VERSE 6:
10. *Love **does not rejoice over another's fault***: Love rejoices in the truth.

VERSE 7:
11. *Love **covers sin***: Love is able to overlook any sin.
12. *Love **always believes the best***: Love looks at facts, not rumors.
13. *Love **always looks on the bright side***: Love is never pessimistic.
14. *Love **sustains us through suffering***: Love remains steadfast in the face of unpleasant circumstances.

VERSE 8:
15. *Love **will never run in defeat***: Love never gives up.

Dr. Tom Constable, (Professor, Emeritus Bible Exposition, Dallas Theological Seminary) sums up 1 Corinthians 13:4-8 like this:

Love does not deal with other people in a way that injures their dignity. It does not insist on having it's own way, nor does it put it's own interest before the needs of others. Love is not irritable or touchy, and it absorbs offenses, insults, and inconveniences for the sake of others' welfare. It does not keep a record of offenses received to pay them back.

The key word in his summary is *absorb*. That is what Jesus did when He was here. He absorbed abuse, rejection, and abandonment for our benefit. He absorbed being mistreated, misrepresented, and misunderstood for our benefit. He could have retaliated against those who wronged Him, but instead He absorbed the shame of the cross so that we may have life eternal. He is our example.

We too should absorb, not argue. We should absorb, not strike back. I am not saying that one should endure physical abuse or any abuse that harms you physically. I am saying that if you behave like love does then you will not argue about anything.

The reason a relationship deteriorates is because we fail to do what God says as discussed in 1 Corinthians 13:4-8. If you behave as love does then you will be patient, always kind and people will feel comfortable in your presence. You will not try to be right in exchange for their feelings, you will not get irritated, you will not draw attention to yourself, and you will not remember a wrong that has been done to you.

If however, you are not loving according to this passage, then you will be impatient, unkind and make others feel uncomfortable. You will insist on being right, draw attention to yourself, get irritated, and store up past wrongs in order to get even. When two people act this way toward each other, of course the relationship will deteriorate.

WHAT CAN YOU DO?

To restore your diminishing relationship, love your mate unconditionally as God loves you. Do not argue, do not get irritated, and do not get angry at your mate. Treat your mate as God treats you…He loves you no matter what you do.

You may be thinking, "I'm not like that all the time." Unfortunately God does not grade us on a sliding scale nor does He give us a free pass. We are to be this kind of person all the time. Can't do it? Allow the Spirit of God to work in your heart to produce this kind of love to share with others, beginning with your mate.

GALATIANS 5:22-23
But the fruit of the Spirit is love, joy, peace, long-suffering, kindness,

goodness, faithfulness, gentleness, self-control. Against such there is no law.

2. FORGIVE FREELY

This is the second way that God treats you. He freely forgives your every sin. Remember, God loved you so much that He forgave you of all your sin when you became a believer.

> **EPHESIANS 4:32**
> *Be kind and compassionate to one another, forgiving each other, just as in Christ, God forgave you.*

What can anyone do to you and me that is greater than what you and I did to Christ? Because of my sin and your sin He went to the cross. What right do you and I have to not forgive someone when Jesus forgave us of much greater sin? There are no conditions or limits to His forgiveness. Every time we sin He is ready to forgive and restore. Not sometimes, but every time!

"How many times should I forgive?" The Apostle Peter was not clear on how much forgiveness should be granted so he asked the Lord:

> **MATTHEW 18:21-22**
> *Then Peter came to Him and said, "Lord, how often shall my brother sin against me, and I forgive him? Up to seven times?" Jesus said to him, "I do not say to you, up to seven times, but up to seventy times seven."*

Peter wanted to appear especially forgiving so he more than doubled what was usually expected and taught by the Jewish rabbis. They thought three was the limit based on Amos 1:3-13 where God forgave Israel's enemies three times and then punished them. Peter probably expected the Lord to commend him for his show of tolerance. Instead Jesus responded that forgiveness should be offered 490 times! Jesus was not saying to stop forgiving after 490, He was saying never stop forgiving. The basis for forgiving others is found in Ephesians 4:32, *"And be kind to one another, tenderhearted, forgiving one another, even as God in Christ forgave you."*

When couples come for counseling, one or both bring with them a lack of love and an unforgiving heart. That's why they sit on opposite ends of the couch. If a couple treated each other the way God treats them, they would love each other unconditionally and forgive each other freely. A relationship will flourish under these conditions and fall apart when these conditions are not met.

Stories abound about the damage that results from not forgiving someone. One lady came to me with three stories. First, she told me of an incident that happened to her when she was five years of age. She told me in great detail how her mother would not let her go outside and play. She asked, and her mother said, "No!" The second story also concerned her mother. When she was ten years of age, she asked her mother if she could ride her horse after school. Her mother said, "No!" The third story once again involved her mother. This time she asked her mother if she could become a school teacher after she graduated from high school. In those days you could teach right after graduation. Her mother's answer was the same as before..."No!" She recalled amazing details as she re-lived each story.

The first incident happened fifty years before. Yes, this lady was fifty-five years of age when she relayed the stories. After listening to her for an hour I mentioned that she was angry at her mother for not allowing her to do those three things. She exploded in anger! She slammed her hand on the desk declaring, "I am not angry at my mother!" There was no meaningful conversation after that and the session ended. Her anger and lack of forgiveness destroyed her relationship with her mother. She also learned to not forgive her husband when she thought he had wronged her. She stayed on medications all of her life and was a frequent visitor to the local mental hospital...all because she would not forgive.

A LACK OF FORGIVENESS IS PRIDE

When a person will not forgive someone it is because of pride. To be prideful is to think more highly of yourself than you ought (Romans 12:3). Remember, no one can do anything to you that is greater than what you and I did to Christ... our sin sent Him to the cross. He has forgiven us so how can you and I do less than forgive others?

> **PROVERBS 16:18**
> *Pride goes before destruction, a haughty spirit before a fall.*

> **ROMANS 12:3**
> *For by the grace given me I say to every one of you: Do not think of yourself more highly than you ought, but rather think of yourself with sober judgment, in accordance with the faith God has distributed to each of you.*

Pride blinds our eyes to the truth that God has forgiven us for every sin we have committed and every sin we will commit. Pride says "How dare you do that to me!" Pride holds on to anger and resentment. Pride looks for a way to get revenge. Grace says, "You're forgiven because I'm forgiven."

> "A proud man is always looking down on things and people; and, of course, as long as you are looking down, you cannot see something that is above you" (C.S. Lewis, *Mere Christianity*).

> "It is better to lose your pride with someone you love rather than to lose that someone you love with your useless pride" (John Ruskin).

WHAT CAN YOU DO?

Stay in your circle now and answer the question, "Have I treated my mate (or others) the way God treats me?" To restore a diminishing relationship, forgive your mate (and others) just as God has forgiven you. Do not argue, do not get irritated, angry, or seek revenge. Treat people as God treats you...He loves you and forgives you no matter what you've done.

3. SHOW GRACE

The third way God treats you is that He shows you grace regardless of what you have done. The concept of grace needs a closer look.

THE MEANING OF GRACE

The Greek word for grace is *charis* and at its core, conveys the sense of favor. It has been said that the word grace is probably the greatest word in the Scriptures because grace is love in action. It can be said that God has, in this one word, revealed His heart toward man.

When God shows His favor to you it is always unearned and always undeserved or it would not be favor. Someone put it this way, "Grace is everything for nothing to those who don't deserve anything." God's greatest demonstration of Grace (favor) is in providing salvation through Jesus Christ.

> **ROMANS 3:23-24**
> *For all have sinned and fall short of the glory of God, being justified freely by His grace through the redemption that is in Christ Jesus.*

EPHESIANS 2:8
For by grace you have been saved through faith, and that not of yourselves; it is the gift of God.

We are to show God's grace (favor) to others. It is easy to show grace to someone that is loving and kind but exceedingly difficult when they are not. Remember your circle? God wants you to show Grace (favor) to your mate even when undeserving. He wants you to be humble and not proud and when you respond this way, He shows you more Grace. Notice James 4:6:

JAMES 4:6 (CEV)
In fact, God treats us with even greater kindness, just as the Scriptures say, "God opposes everyone who is proud, but he is kind to everyone who is humble.

God has freely given His Grace to you in the Person of Jesus Christ. Regardless of what you have done, how mean you have been, or how rebellious you have been, He freely gives His Grace to you, again and again. This is how God treats you and this is how you are to treat other people, starting with your mate.

...AND PETER

There is an amazing truth overlooked in the story of our Lord's crucifixion and resurrection that illustrates Grace (favor). Mark 14:66-72 tells how Peter denied the Lord three times the night before He was crucified.

MARK 14:66-72 (CEV)
While Peter was still in the courtyard, a servant girl of the high priest came up and saw Peter warming himself by the fire. She stared at him and said, "You were with Jesus from Nazareth!" Peter replied, "That isn't true! I don't know what you're talking about. I don't have any idea what you mean." He went out to the gate, and a rooster crowed. The servant girl saw Peter again and said to the people standing there, "This man is one of them!" "No, I'm not!" Peter replied. A little while later some of the people said to Peter, "You certainly are one of them. You're a Galilean!" This time Peter began to curse and swear, "I don't even know the man you're talking about!" Right away the rooster crowed a second time. Then Peter remembered that Jesus had told him, "Before a rooster crows twice, you will say three times that you don't know me." So Peter started crying.

Peter did not want to be identified with Jesus because he was concerned for his own safety. Remember that Peter had witnessed the many miracles that Jesus had performed and he knew that Jesus was God, yet he still denied knowing him out of fear. Peter denied knowing Jesus at His greatest moment of need. Someone has said about the other disciples that they deserted Jesus like rats on a sinking ship. From this incident comes a great truth about living the Spiritual life. In order to grow spiritually you have to be betrayed, denied, and abandoned. These three things happened to Jesus the night before He was crucified.

Three days later Mark records (Mark 16:1), *"Now when the Sabbath was past, Mary Magdalene, Mary the mother of James, and Salome bought spices, that they might come and anoint Him."* When the women arrived at the tomb to anoint Jesus with spices, they discovered that the large stone door had been rolled away (Mark 16:4). When they looked into the tomb they were shocked to see a young man in a white garment sitting on the right side (Mark 16:5). The angel said that Jesus of Nazareth is not here, He is risen! (Mark 16:6). Then, the angel told them to go tell the disciples...and Peter (Mark 16:7)!

What a demonstration of God's Grace (favor)! Peter had denied the Lord three times before He was crucified and God The Father told the angel to tell Mary to be sure to tell Peter that He was risen! God showed Grace to Peter after he betrayed the Lord at His time of need. God shows that same Grace to you and I when we fail Him. Now show the same Grace to others.

If you want to restore your diminishing relationship, show grace to your mate every chance you get. Do not argue, do not get irritated, and do not get angry at your mate. Treat your mate as God treat's you...show grace every chance you get and your relationship will flourish.

GRACE IS CONTAGIOUS

A divorced lady remarried seven years after her husband left her with four children to raise. She had been married to her new husband for less than a year when she found out that he had been unfaithful. She threw all of his clothes in the garage and informed him to get out! She was crying when she called me with the news. She told me the story and added that he was extremely remorseful and pleaded with her to reconsider her decision and begged for forgiveness.

I asked that she treat him like God treats her and to consider extending grace to him. We talked for a long time on the phone and identified some issues that may have contributed to his damaging decision.

The next day she told him of her decision to forgive him. He was shocked that she was willing to forgive him so quickly. They both put the incident behind them and are doing fantastic. It is a testimony to the healing power when the grace of God is shared. But the story does not end here.

The lady's youngest son was dating a girl while in high school and it seemed like a good, long-term match. She suddenly broke off the relationship and as expected, his emotions took a hit. A few weeks passed and she called and wanted to get back together. He was wounded, hurt, and feeling a lot of pain because he really cared for her and even saw them getting married after college. He thought about her request and told his mother, "I'm going to give her a second chance because you gave my step-dad another chance." They are back together and stronger than ever because of grace. The lady extended grace and that encouraged her son to extend grace--grace is contagious!

WHAT CAN YOU DO?

When you extend grace to others, you influence others to do the same and God calls such a person wise:

> **PROVERBS 11:30 (CEV)**
> *Live right, and you will eat from the life-giving tree. And if you act wisely, others will follow.*

To restore a damaged relationship act wisely. Here are four things you can do that reflect love, forgiveness, and grace:

1. NEVER ARGUE

Love does not argue. Arguing is what got you into trouble in the first place. Arguing always takes two people so if you do not participate, there will not be an argument. Consider Proverbs 17:14

> **PROVERBS 17:14 (NIV)**
> *Starting a quarrel is like breaching a dam; so drop the matter before a dispute breaks out.*

2. FORGET THE PAST

Love forgives and forgets. God does not remind us of our sins nor should we remind others of their sins.

> **1 CORINTHIANS 13:5**
> *Love thinks no evil. Love does not keep an account of evil deeds, it forgives.*
>
> **HEBREWS 10:17**
> *Their sins and lawless acts I will remember no more.*

3. BE GRACIOUS

Love is gracious in speech. Always be kind and edifying when you speak. Do not be critical, demeaning, or hurtful with your words. God is very specific in how we are to speak to others in Ephesians 4:29-32. The CEV captures clearly what to say and what not to say. If two people who are having difficulty in their relationship choose to follow this guide, their relationship would immediately improve and even flourish.

> **EPHESIANS 4:29-32 (CEV)**
> *Stop all your dirty talk. Say the right thing at the right time and help others by what you say. Don't make God's Spirit sad. The Spirit makes you sure that someday you will be free from your sins. Stop being bitter and angry and mad at others. Don't yell at one another or curse each other or ever be rude. Instead, be kind and merciful, and forgive others, just as God forgave you because of Christ.*

4. FIND SOMETHING TO LAUGH ABOUT EVERYDAY

People who argue look for evidence to support their position and fail to be loving, forgiving and gracious. One who is loving, forgiving, and gracious will have a "happy heart" according to Proverbs. Here are two passages to consider:

> **PROVERBS 15:13**
> *A merry heart makes a cheerful countenance: but by sorrow of the heart the spirit is broken.*

> **PROVERBS 15:15**
> *For the despondent, every day brings trouble; for the happy heart, life is a continual feast.*

If you do not argue, if you do not bring up past issues, if you are gracious in how you talk to your mate, and you find something to laugh about every day then you are dealing with your circle and God will bless you and your relationships.

SUMMARY

The important relationships in our lives deteriorate or fail because we do not do what God has told us to do. To repair a damaged relationship, treat others the way God treats you. He loves you unconditionally, He forgives you freely, and He showers you with His grace (favor).

You can only be responsible for yourself--that's your circle. Actually, that's all God expects of you. Do your part regardless of what your mate (or another person) does. Love unconditionally, forgive freely, and show grace (favor) every chance you get.

Ask God to do His work in you so that you can become an example of a loving, forgiving, and gracious person. Depend on Him to give you the strength to become this kind of person. Ask Him to develop these qualities in you. Pray that your mate will respond the same. Remember, do not be concerned about what your mate does or does not do. You can only be responsible for yourself--stay in your circle.

"Don't judge someone else because their sin is different than yours."

ANNETTE SAFSTROM

part three
MENTAL DISORDERS

eight

DO I HAVE A MENTAL DISORDER?
The Medical Model

Some Christians seek counseling because they believe, or have been told, that they have a mental disorder. Many have already been put on medication to treat their symptoms. The most common diagnosis that I have worked with are anxiety, depression, and bipolar disorder.

What mental-health professionals call mental disorder or a mental illness (these terms are used interchangeably) is considered to be a deviation from normal behavior. The Oxford English Dictionary defines normal as "conforming to a standard." Each society identifies behavior that within that society is considered acceptable or unacceptable. Normal behavior is therefore relative to standards of the society in which it is found. Those who have behavior that does not conform to the accepted norm in their society would be classified as abnormal and would therefore invite a sanction (diagnosis)--attaching a stigma of a "mental disorder."

The Medical Model states simply that abnormal behavior is a medical condition in the brain that can be treated with medications. Here is how The National Alliance on Mental Illness defines mental illness:

> A mental illness is a medical condition that disrupts a person's thinking, feeling, mood, ability to relate to others and daily functioning. Just as diabetes is a disorder of the pancreas, mental illnesses are medical conditions that often result in a diminished capacity for coping with the ordinary demands of life.
>
> Serious mental illnesses include major depression, schizophrenia, bipolar disorder, obsessive compulsive disorder (OCD), panic disorder, post-traumatic stress disorder (PTSD) and borderline personality disorder. The good news about mental illness is that recovery is possible.
>
> Mental illnesses can affect persons of any age, race, religion or income. Mental illnesses are not the result of personal weakness, lack of character or poor upbringing. Mental illnesses are treatable. Most

people diagnosed with a serious mental illness can experience relief from their symptoms by actively participating in an individual treatment plan.

According to WebMD, there are two areas that are targeted to explain the cause of a mental illness within the medical model:

HEREDITY (GENETICS)

Many mental illnesses run in families, suggesting they may be passed on from parents to children through genes. Genes contain instructions for the function of each cell in the body and are responsible for how we look, act, think, etc. However, just because your mother or father may have or had a mental illness doesn't mean you will have one. Hereditary just means that you are more likely to get the condition than if you didn't have an affected family member. Experts believe that many mental conditions are linked to problems in multiple genes—not just one, as with many diseases—which is why a person inherits a susceptibility to a mental disorder but doesn't always develop the condition. The disorder itself occurs from the interaction of these genes and other factors—such as psychological trauma and environmental stressors—which can influence, or trigger, the illness in a person who has inherited a susceptibility to it.

BIOLOGY

Some mental illnesses have been linked to an abnormal balance of brain chemicals called neurotransmitters. Neurotransmitters help nerve cells in the brain communicate with each other. If these chemicals are out of balance or are not working properly, messages may not make it through the brain correctly, leading to symptoms of mental illness.

Joseph Carver (2009) in the article, *The Chemical Imbalance in Mental Health Problems* comments on common neurotransmitters:

Neurological research has identified over fifty (50) neurotransmitters in the brain. Research also tells us that several neurotransmitters are related to mental health problems–Dopamine, Serotonin, Norepinephrine, and GABA (Gamma Aminobutyric Acid). Too much or too little of these neurotransmitters are now felt to produce psychiatric conditions...This simply and commonly used explanation recognizes that the condition is a medical problem and that it can be treated with medication. The 'chemical imbalance' explanation also reflects the overall theme of treatment–identifying what neurotransmitters are involved in the clinical symptom picture and with medication, attempting to return that neurotransmitter level back to the 'normal range'.

SUMMARY

The medical model considers behavior that is outside society's accepted norm as an illness caused either by genetic inheritance or faulty brain chemistry. The proponents of the medical model conclude that although the exact causes of mental illnesses are not known, it is definitely not personal weakness. This view promotes that recovery from a mental illness is not simply a matter of will and self-discipline.

EVALUATION OF THE MEDICAL MODEL

Let's take a closer look at the two areas that are claimed to be the causes of or contributor to a mental disorder (mental illness); genetics and chemical imbalance. Environmental influences will be addressed in the next chapter.

GENETICS

This is the theory is that there are "personality genes" (both good and bad) that are passed on to us that contain the markers of a mental disorder and may develop under certain circumtances.

A favorite target of researchers is identifying the gene that produces schizophrenia. Dr. Colin Ross and Alvin Pam comment on the research on the so-called schizophrenic gene in *Pseudoscience in Biological Psychiatry: Blaming The Body*, "The belief that schizophrenia is a specific organic disease or a group of organic brain diseases has never been confirmed. We have been on the verge of confirming it since the dawn of modern psychiatry, and we are still on the verge" (Ross & Pam, 1994, pp. 193-194).

Michael W. Kraus, Ph.D., reviewed the genetic research and concluded, "The current prevailing genetic evidence seems to suggest that we actually don't have genes for personality" (Kraus, 2013).

CHEMICAL IMBALANCE

The chemical imbalance theory has become so widely accepted that it is assumed to be true and not questioned as to factual validity; it is presented as scientific fact. However, those who accept the chemical imbalance cause of mental disorders must answer two questions:

1. WHAT IS A NORMAL CHEMICAL BALANCE IN THE BRAIN?

No one knows what a "normal range" is for these neurotransmitters which is a fundamental flaw in the theory. You cannot return something to its proper level when the proper level is not known. The imbalance theory is worthless unless the balance is known.

2. HOW CAN IT BE DETERMINED THAT BRAIN CHEMISTRY IS OUT-OF-BALANCE?

In order to determine whether or not one has a "chemical imbalance," laboratory work needs to be done. However, there are no blood tests administered to determine the current levels of the neurotransmitters. How then can it be determined that there is a chemical imbalance without scientific evidence showing the imbalance? No scientific evidence is ever collected before a person is given a diagnosis and offered medication.

The chemical imbalance theory is considered to be the *most* scientific of all the theories to explain abnormal behavior. The fact is that it is the *least* scientific because no physical evidence is collected to support a conclusion.

The reason the diagnosis of anxiety, depression, and bipolar (or other disorders) are not determined by a blood test is because no such tests are available. When symptoms such as feeling blue, an inability to sleep, or having emotional highs and lows are reported, medication is offered. Virtually all disorders that are said to be caused by a chemical imbalance are determined *only* after hearing these kind of symptoms *without one piece of physical evidence from the patient.* Blood tests are given *after* medication is administered to determine the levels of the drugs ingested.

AN IRRESPONSIBLE DIAGNOSIS?

I went to my doctor years ago to get an explanation of an event that had occurred a few days earlier. I explained that I suddenly became confused, disoriented, I broke out in a cold sweat, and my vision became blurry. I was unable to continue driving safely so I pulled into a parking lot. I thought my blood sugar had dropped and I needed some orange juice. Fortunately, there was a grocery store near where I had parked. It took about twenty minutes before I could gain enough control to go into the store and get sugar into my system. Still a bit disoriented, it took about ten minutes of wandering around in the store before I finally found the orange juice. I drank it quickly and then paid the clerk. I slowly regained my senses and was able to continue safely on my way.

After only hearing my symptoms, my doctor of ten years looked at me and said, "I have some bad news for you, you have a tumor on your pancreas!" I was stunned! My first thought was that I had cancer and I had three months to live and said to myself, "Lord I'm coming home." He then said he wanted a second opinion and walked out of the room to phone a colleague. At that very moment my brother called. I told him that the doctor had just informed me that I had a tumor on my pancreas and that I likely had only three months to live! I said that I would call him back. I sat there lonely and numb. I had three months to live, who survives pancreatic cancer? After what seemed like hours the doctor returned to the examination room (actually about fifteen minutes). He said, "I lied, you have Hypoglycemia!"

After hearing my symptoms, my doctor made his diagnosis. He did not suggest scanning for a tumor on my pancreas, or giving me a glucose tolerance test, or giving me a blood test. Was he irresponsible? Many would say that he was. Medical doctors are to gather sufficient physical evidence before declaring a diagnosis--especially a potentially life-ending diagnosis.

OPPOSITION TO THE CHEMICAL IMBALANCE THEORY

Although it is presented by medical doctors, psychologists, counselors and the media that the chemical imbalance theory is scientific, not all agree. Do an Internet search on the topic of chemical imbalance and you will see the level of opposition against this theory. Here is what four psychiatrists have to say about the chemical imbalance theory.

DR. COLIN ROSS-PSYCHIATRIST

Dr. Ross states in *Pseudoscience In Biological Psychiatry: Blaming The Body*, "The inherent bias in a reductionistic biological psychiatry is that no one—not even the afflicted individual—is accountable for his or her behavior, because abnormal behavior is presumed to have some pathophysiological cause" (Ross & Pham, 1994, p.6)

Dr. Ross raised the question about blaming the body for behavior, "The question is never asked as to whether the body can indeed cause rather than mediate a psychiatric symptom—as if the body, which actualizes what we do, also tells us how to live" (p. 9).

Dr. Ross states further, "Despite vigorous laboratory investigation, no psychiatric disorder has thus far been cured by medication, not even manic disorder where lithium treatment has been so helpful. The efficacy of a drug does not prove that a particular mental disturbance is biochemically determined. For example, aspirin relieves headaches but no one contends that a headache is brought about by aspirin deficiency" (p. 41).

DR. PETER R. BREGGIN-PSYCHIATRIST

Perhaps the strongest and most aggressive voice against biological psychiatry comes from Peter R. Breggin, M.D., a psychiatrist since the late 1960's. He writes, "In summary, the neurolepic drugs are chemical lobotomizing agents with no specific therapeutic effect on any symptom or problems. Their main impact is to blunt and subdue the individual." He goes on to say, "Thus they [psychiatric drugs] produce a chemical lobotomy and a chemical straitjacket. Indeed, there is relatively little evidence that they are helpful to the patients themselves, while there is considerable evidence that psychosocial interventions are much better" (Breggin, 1994, p. 67).

Dr. Breggin states, "Since the antidepressants frequently make people feel worse, since they interfere with both psychotherapy and spontaneous improvement by blunting the emotions and confusing the mind, since most are easy tools for suicide, since they have many adverse physical side effects, since they can be difficult to withdraw from, and since there's little evidence for their effectiveness-- it makes sense never to use them" (Breggin, 1994, p. 171).

Dr. Breggin and Cohen states in *Your Drug May Be your Problem: How and Why To Stop Taking Psychiatric Medications*, "Psychiatric medications are, first and foremost, psychoactive or psychotropic drugs. They influence the way a person feels, thinks, and acts. Like cocaine and heroin, they change the emotional response capacity of the brain. If used to solve emotional problems, they end up shoving those problems under the rug of drug intoxication while creating additional drug-induced problems" (Breggin & Cohen, 1999, p. 12).

Between 2012-2013 Dr. Peter Breggin published a video series on Simple Truths About Psychiatry. In the first of the series, "Do You Have a Biochemical Imbalance" he states simply that a chemical imbalance does not exist until the medication is administered (available at www.breggin.com).

DR. WILLIAM GLASSER-PSYCHIATRIST

Dr. Glasser (2003) makes the following statement in his book, *Warning: Psychiatry Can Be Hazardous to Your Mental Health*:

> The medical approach to mental distress is based on unproven hypotheses, in particular the theory that the fundamental cause of mental distress is biological, either a biochemical imbalance, a genetic defect, or both. Psychiatry has convinced itself and the general public that this hypothesis is not a hypothesis but a proven fact. In doing so, modem psychiatry has made a major error of judgment, an error so fundamental that it should never occur in any discipline purporting to be scientific. But psychiatry gets away with it, because instead of policing psychiatry to ensure that it does not lose the run of itself, legislators and the general public alike place great faith and trust in the integrity and objectivity of psychiatry and psychiatric research. What limited policing there is of psychiatry is not in-depth and relies heavily on the bona fides [good faith, sincerity] of psychiatrists and medical researchers.
>
> Decades of intensive psychiatric research have failed to establish a biological cause for any psychiatric condition. The lack of biological evidence is confirmed by the extraordinary fact that not a single psychiatric diagnosis can be confirmed by a biochemical, radiological, or other laboratory test. I know of no other medical specialty where vast numbers of people are treated on the presumption of a biochemical abnormality. The medical profession's reliance on biology as the determining factor for psychiatric disorders is founded upon faith rather than true scientific research. It seems to me that doctors shoot in the dark far more than the public realizes. And despite all you have heard, little real progress has been made in the research on the genetics of mental illness. As the Chicago Tribune stated on March 20, 2001: "It is a fact that despite decades of research, not a single gene responsible for mental illness has been found—the quest has been shattered by the debunking of highly visible reports localizing genes for schizophrenia. Similar fates met discoveries of genes for manic-depression, alcoholism, and homosexuality."

DR. THOMAS SZASZ-PSYCHIATRIST

Dr. Thomas Szasz (1920-2012) wrote *The Myth of Mental Illness*. Thomas H.

Maugh II wrote an article about Szasz's work which appeared in the Los Angeles Times newspaper on September 17, 2012. Here are excerpts from that article.

> He argued that mental illness wasn't a disease but "problems in living." He called for an end to using drugs to treat psychiatric disorders. His attacks on the psychiatric profession in the 1960s and 1970s led him to a position of prominence and influence before his radical ideas fell into disrepute and he faded into obscurity. He argued against using drugs to treat mental disorders, using insanity as a defense against criminal acts and committing' people to mental institutions against their will. He called the latter act "a crime against humanity."
>
> He said, "I am probably the only psychiatrist in the world whose hands are clean. I have never committed anyone. I have never given electric shock. I have never, ever given drugs to a mental patient."
>
> He argued, "that the vast, majority of psychiatric diagnoses were ill-conceived and scientifically baseless."

DR. THEODORE DALRYMPLE-PSYCHIATRIST

Bad Behavior isn't an Illness is the title of an article written by Theodore Dalrymple and published in the Los Angeles Times, November 5, 2013. The article is a critique of the DSM-5 (*Diagnostic and Statistical Manual of Mental Disorders-5*). This is the psychiatrist's catalog of all behavior that is classified as a mental disorder or so-called mental disease. Dr. Dalrymple challenges the DSM-5's classification of the diagnosis of Intermittent Explosive Disorder. Here are excerpts from the article.

> The manual that psychiatrist's use to diagnose mental disorders is too quick to classify moral lapses as full-blown pathologies...Yet the new DSM-5 does agree with abused women that their male abusers are suffering from a psychiatric condition: intermittent explosive disorder.
>
> Is the habit of losing one's temper and destroying things or hurting people really a medical condition? Doesn't the diagnosis empty the act both of meaning and moral content, all in the service of a spurious objectivity? The notion of an outburst of temper grossly out of proportion to whatever provoked it—a factor necessary to the diagnosis—implies moral judgment as to what constitutes appropriate and inappropriate displays of anger. Appropriateness is an irreducibly moral concept, requiring conscious judgment; no number of functional MRI scans of the amygdala or of any other part of the brain will assist

in that judgment...no objective laboratory markers or correlatives of psychiatric disorder exist...the DSM-5 does establish its authors' lack of common sense, the quality that psychiatrists, perhaps more than any other kind of doctor, need. The manual's lack of common sense would be amusing were it not destined to be taken with superstitious seriousness by psychiatrists around the world, as well as by insurers and lawyers.

Psychiatry has gone too far trying to explain behavior that they have decided is outside the acceptable norm in our society. Actually, acceptable behavior is being reduced by the frequent addition of new diagnosis in the DSM revisions.

To illustrate how absurd it has become, they are now attempting to call ordinary daydreaming and mind-wandering in children a disorder called sluggish cognitive tempo (SCT)! The following excerpt is from an article by Alan Schwartz that was published in the New York Times newspaper April 11, 2014; "Idea of New Attention Disorder Spurs Research, and Debate."

> Yet now some powerful figures in mental health are claiming to have identified a new disorder that could vastly expand the ranks of young people treated for attention problems. Called sluggish cognitive tempo, the condition is said to be characterized by lethargy, daydreaming and slow mental processing. By some researchers' estimates, it is present in perhaps two million children.
>
> "I have no doubt there are kids who meet the criteria for this thing, but nothing is more irrelevant," Dr. Frances said. The enthusiasts here are thinking of missed patients. What about the mislabeled kids who are called patients when there's nothing wrong with them? They are not considering what is happening in the real world.

The real world is made up of parents that recognize that children are born with different personalities or natural tendencies (temperament). Some are extroverts and some are introverts. Some children are easy to raise and others are not. Extroverts are easily distracted and they need lots of activity. Introverts adapt to their environment, not wanting to be disruptive. There are common sense reasons why children daydream or their mind drifts around while in a classroom. They could just be bored or not interested in the subject. They just might have a boring teacher.

If we continue down this path that modern psychiatry is leading us, we will soon lose the ability to identify what is normal behavior. In 1969 the song "In The Year 2525" written by Richard Lee Evans was number one for six weeks.

Here are the opening words of the song sung by Zager and Evans:

> In the year 2525,
> If man is still alive,
> If woman can survive,
> They may find-
> In the year 3535
> Ain't gonna need to tell the truth,
> Tell no lies.
> Everything you think, do, and say
> Is in the pill you took today.

These words were written in 1969 and were not meant to be prophetic but nearly 50 years later look where we are headed.

AN ERRANT PATH

The following illustrations shows just how far our society has gone to excuse behavior because of the influence of psychiatry. The incident happened near Fort Worth, Texas in June, 2013. A sixteen year old boy acknowledged that he was drunk on alcohol and Valium when he lost control of his speeding pickup truck and slammed into a broken-down car, killing four people. His attorneys claimed he had been spoiled by his parents and was never taught right from wrong or a sense of responsibility; a term one witness dubbed "affluenza." He was sentenced to 10 years' probation. No jail time. This is an inconceivable conclusion because it removes the boy from the consequences of the choices he willfully made.

This is the result of psychiatry promoting that behavior is determined by something other than the individual making choices. In their view, no one is actually responsible for their own behavior since genetics, and faulty brain chemistry contribute to or cause behavior. And the above case establishes that if you are not raised appropriately, then you are not accountable for your choices. As a result, absurd, irresponsible, and mind numbing statements are made like "Mental illnesses are not the result of personal weakness, lack of character, or poor upbringing."

SUMMARY

The two areas identified as causing or contributing to so-called mental disorders do not survive close investigation. The genetic connection has not been established and the chemical imbalance theory cannot be proven scientifically.

The field of psychiatry has labeled common and ordinary sadness over a loss as depression and medication is offered. Hyperactive children are labeled ADD or ADHD and medicated. Natural shyness is labeled as a social phobia. Severe mood shifts are explained as a chemical imbalance in the brain and given the label of bipolar. Typical anxiety is also identified as a condition requiring medication. There has been a hostile takeover by psychiatry for behavior that can be explained another way other than by genetics and a chemical imbalance.

nine

DO I HAVE A MENTAL DISORDER?
Environmental Influences

Some theories look to the environment to identify causes of mental disorders. These may include family dynamics; psychological stressors; sexual abuse; substance abuse; physical abuse; a lack of employment opportunities; etc.

The environmental view is closely related to a non-medical theory of behavior called Behaviorism. This theory teaches that all behavior, appropriate or inappropriate, is the result of conditioning by the environment.

This view fails to accept that an individual makes a choice as to how they respond to their environment. A dysfunctional or abusive environment however, does not automatically require that a person respond with a negative lifestyle attitude, or develop extreme, irresponsible behavior. No one has to look far to find someone that decided not be influenced by a difficult or abusive environment. It is also easy to find someone that came from a healthy environment and decided to be irresponsible. It is not the environment, it is a person's *response* to their environment that matters most.

VICTOR FRANKL

Viktor Frankl's inspiring story is a superb illustration of what a person can do in an unthinkable environment. Frankl (1905-1997) was the originator of Logotherapy. Every time I heard Dr. Bob Burns, President of the Viktor Frankl Institute of Logotherapy, tell Frankl's story at Logotherapy conferences, I have been overwhelmed at what he experienced and his response to unimaginable horror.

Viktor Frankl was a Jewish psychiatrist during WWII. The Germans took him and his family to three different concentration camps, the worse being Auschwitz. While there, everyone in his family (except his sister) died, including his wife who was pregnant. Many prisoners died, overwhelmed by the trauma and tragedy of the concentration camp. Dr. Frankl survived and wrote a book about his experience, *Man's Search For Ultimate Meaning*, one of the ten most popular books ever written. Everyone should read this book.

Dr. Frankl teaches that anything can be taken away from you, including the things you have and the people you love. However, the right and freedom you have to choose the attitude about what is happening to you cannot be taken away from you. One of the ten tenants of his Logotherapy is as follows: "Individuals are not products of their parents; they are absolutely new. We are not products of our past nor victims of it. We are the results of our choices and responses to what has happened to us."

WILLIAM GLASSER

William Glasser, M.D., has written several books that reflect individual responsibility and accountability. In 1984 he wrote *Take Effective Control of Your Life*, and in 1998 he wrote *Choice Theory*. Dr. Glasser is also convinced that it is not forces outside of us that have control; it is that which is within that determines our behavior. He says in *Take Effective Control of Your Life*:

> We are motivated completely by forces inside ourselves, and all of our behavior is our attempt to control our own lives. When, for example, we blame our misery on a child, spouse, or parent, we are acting as if they, not we, are in control of our lives (Glasser, pp. xiii-xiv, 1984).

> Nothing we do is caused by what happens outside of us. If we believe that what we do is caused by forces outside of us we are acting like dead machines, not living people. Because we are alive we can choose whether or not to answer the phone, depending on whether or not it fulfills a current goal (Glasser, pp. 1-2, 1984).

IS THE ENVIRONMENT CAUSAL?

Environmental psychology looks to a person's environment to explain behavior as if the individual has no part in their response to the environment. I am not saying that a person's environment cannot influence a person's behavior, I am saying that people choose to respond to their environment the way they do. As Dr. Glasser pointed out, we are controlled by forces *inside* us and not forces from the *outside*. The environment *cannot* cause a person to respond positively or negatively. It is always the individual's choice. Since we are thinking and feeling human beings it is understandable that when faced with a negative even abusive environment that many choose to be fearful, withdraw, or run away. Not all, however, respond this way.

If the environment has causal power, then we have a difficult time explaining what Satan and Adam did in their perfect environments. Satan was created and given free will and was in the presence of Almighty God. In that perfect environment Satan still made a choice to rebel against God. He was in a perfect environment but was not influenced by the presence of God. After God created the universe He then created Adam and Eve. They were in a perfect environment and spoke directly to God every day. To them it was normal to speak to God and actually hear His voice. Yet in that perfect environment what did they do? They choose to rebel against God's authority. It is not the environment, it is a person's *response* to their environment that matters most.

ILLUSTRATIONS FROM THE BIBLE

The Bible does not allow for anyone to excuse their behavior because of environmental influences.

JOSEPH

Consider Joseph's story as recorded in Genesis 37:1-50:26. Joseph was favored by his father and hated by his brothers. The brothers threw him in a pit and wanted him to die! Then they sold him as a slave to a group headed for Egypt. Joseph eventually became the second most powerful man in Egypt and was faithful to his master by rejecting his wife's advances. Because he resisted her, Joseph was imprisoned under false charges. Eventually, there was a famine in his homeland and it brought his brothers to Egypt looking for food. Joseph had the perfect opportunity to get revenge but instead he showed them love and forgiveness and they were reconciled as a family.

It is fair to say that Joseph did not have a good environment in which to grow and develop. In spite of what he experienced his response was (Genesis 50:20), *"But as for you, you meant evil against me; but God meant it for good, in order to bring it about as it is this day, to save many people alive."*

JOB

Job lost his family, his health, and his wealth. His wife tried to give him some much needed direction *"Then his wife said to him, 'Do you still hold fast to your integrity? Curse God and die!'"* (Job 2:9). His friends were no better (Job 4-11 and 32-37). Yet Job said *"Though He slay me, yet will I trust Him. Even so, I will defend my own ways before Him"* (Job 13:15).

Job's environment was great in the beginning but took a turn for the worst. He had every opportunity to be permanently bitter about his life's events but he saw God's hand in everything that happened.

EPHESIANS

Ephesians 5 and 6 covers relationships for husbands and wives, parents and children, and masters and slaves: husbands are to love their wives, wives are to submit to their husbands, children are to obey their parents, fathers are not to provoke their children to anger, and servants are to obey their masters. God's ideal environment for a family includes love, obedience, submission, and respect for each other. When this does not happen, people often grow up wounded, scared, and stuck in their pain. Remember the lady who's mother refused to let her do three things (see page 52) The environment was toxic for that young girl and she allowed it to mark her for the rest of her life.

SUMMARY

Events in an environment cannot cause a person to have a response that is either positive or negative. Everyone chooses their response to the events in their environment.

ten

THE BIBLICAL VIEW OF BEHAVIOR

The task of all who study human behavior is to explain why people do what they do. A theory of behavior represents a set of beliefs that attempts to identify the cause of normal, abnormal, or even extreme behavior. As discussed, psychiatrists believe that behavior is based on an individual's genetic inheritance or their brain chemistry balance. Others look at environmental influences for causes of behavior.

These models of behavior teach that an individual is not the cause of nor are they responsible for their behavior, rather, they are victims of genetics, faulty brain chemistry, or environmental influences. Our society has been so conditioned to believe the *victim* position that to suggest otherwise, is viewed as simplistic or heresy.

Since the previously discussed positions cannot survive scrutiny, we are left to find another explanation for behavior including maladaptive behavior. We need to look no further than the Bible:

2 TIMOTHY 3:16
All Scripture is given by inspiration of God, and is profitable for doctrine, for reproof, for correction, for instruction in righteousness.

All we need to explain behavior (both good and bad) is what God has given us in His Word. The Scripture contains what is true and will help us realize what we are doing that is wrong and then tells us the right thing to do. Let's consider what the Bible says about behavior.

BEHAVIOR IS A CHOICE

Humans are made in the image or likeness of God which means we think, we feel, and we choose. Our mind represents intelligence that gives us the ability to think, reason, form ideas, create, communicate, and relate to others. Our emotions allow us to feel excitement and sadness and they enable us to enjoy life and identify with the conditions of others. Our free will enables us to make choices that are either good or bad.

Throughout the Bible, God consistently tells us what to do and not do. He gave us the Ten Commandments (Exodus 20) and the Law and expected obedience (nine are repeated in the New Testament). He told us what would happen if there was obedience and what would happen if there wasn't (Deuteronomy 28). The new Testament is loaded with directives to *do* this and *not do* that, to *put on* and to *put off* certain behaviors (Ephesians 4). The presence of commands and directives throughout Scripture means that since we have free will we can obey or not obey. It's a choice.

What we learned from Adam and Eve's response is obvious, each time their behavior reflected a willful choice. Since they were the first humans, there were no "disorder genes" they inherited that caused their behavior, nor did God excuse their choices by saying that it was their brain's fault. Two sinless human beings in a perfect environment made a choice to disobey God's clear and direct command.

They both made a *choice* to hide what they had done by covering themselves with aprons they hastily made from fig leaves (Genesis 3:7). When they heard God's voice in the garden, they became frightened and chose to hide among the trees because of fear. God then asked a question (Genesis 3:9) to which He knew the answer, "Adam, where are you?" God was not looking for an answer, He was looking for a confession. Adam and Eve instead, chose to rationalize and blame shift their responsibility.

OUTSIDE INFLUENCES

The Spirit of God influenced behavior in the Old Testament (Gideon in Judges 6:34; Jephthah in Judges 11:29; Samson in Judges 14:6,19; 15:14), and permanently indwells Christians in the New Testament (Ephesians 4:30).

Satan and demonic influence, including possession, can alter a person's state (1 Samuel 16:14-15; 18:10-11; 19:9-10; Matthew 12:32-33; 17:14-18; Mark 5:1-20; 7:26-30; Luke 4:33-36; Acts 16:16-18). In the cases of demonic influence, the individual still makes a choice. In Luke 22:3-4 Satan entered Judas and he influenced him to betray Jesus.

The Spirit of God, Satan and his demons, and environment can influence the choices a person makes as noted. That being said, the *emphasis* in the Bible centers on individual responsibility to choose to obey the Scripture's directives and commands:

JOSHUA 24:15
And if it seems evil to you to serve the Lord, choose for yourselves this day whom you will serve, whether the gods which your fathers served that were on the other side of the River, or the gods of the Amorites, in whose land you dwell. But as for me and my house, we will serve the Lord.

BEHAVIOR HAS CONSEQUENCES

Consequences followed Adam and Eve's choice to disobey God (Genesis 3:14-24). Notice the order in which God dealt with the serpent, the woman, and Adam:

1. The serpent (Satan used the serpent as his vessel) would not only crawl on it's belly but it (Satan) would one day be defeated by Jesus Christ (Genesis 3:14-15).

2. The woman would have pain in child birth and be subject to her husband (Genesis 3:16).

3. Adam would sweat to grow food from a cursed ground and he would return to the dust from which he was made. Adam and Eve were then thrown out of the garden where God had provided everything for them (Genesis 3:17-24). Paradise was lost.

BEHAVIOR REVEALS THE HEART

The heart in the Bible is considered the seat of the mind, emotions, and will. In Matthew 15:18-20 Jesus identified some behaviors that come out of a person's heart:

MATTHEW 15:18-20
But those things which proceed out of the mouth come from the heart, and they defile a man. For out of the heart proceed evil thoughts, murders, adulteries, fornications, thefts, false witness, blasphemies. These are the things which defile a man, but to eat with unwashed hands does not defile a man.

In Proverbs 9:8-9 Solomon tells us that a person's heart is revealed in how they respond to correction:

PROVERBS 9:8-9
Do not correct a scoffer, lest he hate you; Rebuke a wise man, and he will love you. Give instruction to a wise man, and he will be still wiser; Teach a just man, and he will increase in learning.

BEHAVIOR INFLUENCES OTHERS

Your example matters to someone. We typically live our lives without this awareness, but someone is watching and being influenced by what you do. It matters how you treat servers at restaurants, clerks in department stores, your mate, your children, your friends, your co-workers, your girlfriend, or boyfriend. Every encounter with another human matters. You can make a good impression or a bad impression--every time it matters.

GOOD INFLUENCE

PROVERBS 11:30 (CEV)
Live right, and you will eat from the life-giving tree. And if you act wisely, others will follow.

BAD INFLUENCE

PROVERBS 22:24-25 (CEV)
Don't make friends with anyone who has a bad temper. You might turn out like them and get caught in a trap.

To be a good influence on others and have a positive impact, you must first be an example of the person the psalmists describes in Psalms 1:1-3:

PSALMS 1:1-3
Blessed is the man who walks not in the counsel of the ungodly, Nor stands in the path of sinners, nor sits in the seat of the scornful; but his delight is in the law of the Lord, and in His law he meditates day and night. He shall be like a tree planted by the rivers of water, that brings forth its fruit in its season, whose leaf also shall not wither; and whatever he does shall prosper.

BEHAVIOR MUST BE CONTROLLED

We were given free will but that does not mean we can do what we want to do when we want to do it. God expects us to exercise self-control. Self-control is so important that it is included in the fruit of the Spirit listed in Galatians 5:22-24, *"But the fruit of the Spirit is love, joy, peace, long-suffering, kindness, goodness, faithfulness, gentleness, self-control. Against such there is no law. And those who are Christ's have crucified the flesh with its passions and desires."*

A lack of self-control can lead to difficulties in virtually every area of a person's life. When a person lacks self-control they get angry, talk too much, eat too much, drink too much, sleep too much, and fail to control their emotions. These excesses in behavior are what must be controlled and avoided.

CONTROLLING YOUR ANGER

Proverbs 16:32 says that self-control is more valuable than physical strength, *"He who is slow to anger is better than the mighty, And he who rules his spirit than he who takes a city."* This proverb contrasts self-control (rule your spirit and do not get angry) to being able to take (capture) a city. The word translated "take" actually means more than to just capture, it holds the meaning *to occupy*. The conclusion is that it is better to have self-control (don't get angry) than to be so powerful that you alone could overtake and occupy a city. Such external power is not to be compared to the internal power of self-control. This proverb is talking about being more concerned about controlling yourself rather than controlling others (or even occupying a city).

CONTROLLING YOUR SPEECH

These proverbs are saying that the more you talk, the more likely you will say something you regret. The less you say reflects wisdom. The word translated as "restrains" in Proverbs 10:19 means *to refuse*. In order to refuse means that one is aware of what they are doing and makes a choice not to speak. One lady told me that she was continually getting herself into trouble because she was not able to control her tongue! What she was really saying was she was not willing to control what she said.

> **PROVERBS 10:19**
> *In the multitude of words sin is not lacking, But he who restrains his lips is wise.*

> **PROVERBS 17:27-28**
> *He who has knowledge spares his words, And a man of understanding is of a calm spirit. Even a fool is counted wise when he holds his peace; When he shuts his lips, he is considered perceptive.*

CONTROLLING YOUR APPETITE

Controlling ones appetite for food and drink can be challenging for some and exceedingly difficult for others. Some even use food or drink to bury emotional pain. Regardless of why one abuses food and drink the following proverbs are a warning that if you overeat and abuse wine you will lose everything you have.

> **PROVERBS 23:20-21**
> *Be not among drunkards or among gluttonous eaters of meat, for the drunkard and the glutton will come to poverty, and slumber will clothe them with rags.*

CONTROLLING DRINKING

This next proverb teaches that drinking can bring pleasure but in excess it is addictive and destructive. See also, Ephesians 5:18, Galatians 5:21, and Proverbs 23:20-21.

> **PROVERBS 23:29-35**
> *Who has woe? Who has sorrow? Who has contentions? Who has complaints? Who has wounds without cause? Who has redness of eyes? Those who linger long at the wine, Those who go in search of mixed wine. Do not look on the wine when it is red, When it sparkles in the cup, When it swirls around smoothly; At the last it bites like a serpent, And stings like a viper. Your eyes will see strange things, And your heart will utter perverse things. Yes, you will be like one who lies down in the midst of the sea, Or like one who lies at the top of the mast, saying: "They have struck me, but I was not hurt; They have beaten me, but I did not feel it. When shall I awake, that I may seek another drink?*

Some Christians use "there are demons within me" to explain why they are alcohol and drug addicts. We overlook the fact that every person inherited the sin nature from Adam and every person is capable of sinful choices without the influence of Satan or his demons. Galatians 5:22-24 is teaching that if you walk in the Spirit, selfish feelings and desires (like alcohol and drugs) will not have power over you.

CONTROLLING HOW MUCH YOU SLEEP

Everyone needs sleep but not everyone needs the same amount of sleep. Most would agree that an average of somewhere around eight hours is sufficient for most people. Some function well on much less. The Scripture does warn, however, about sleeping too much. Such a person is called a *sluggard* as noted in the following Proverbs and will likely end up in poverty because they will not work.

> **PROVERBS 6:9**
> *How long will you slumber, O sluggard? When will you rise from your sleep?"*

> **PROVERBS 20:13**
> *Do not love sleep, lest you come to poverty; Open your eyes, and you will be satisfied with bread..*

CONTROLLING YOUR EMOTIONS

> **PROVERBS 29:11**
> *A fool vents all his feelings, but a wise man holds them back.*

The Scripture does not speak kindly of one who does not control their *negative* emotions. The word translated "fool" can mean *foolish, silly, and even stupid*. By contrast, a person is called wise when they control their emotions. The word "wise" can be translated *intelligent*, which is in contrast to *stupid* used in the first part of this proverb. The Scripture is clear, *we are to be in control of our emotions*.

BEHAVIOR WILL BE REWARDED OR PUNISHED

All behavior will be examined by Christ and either rewarded at the Judgment Seat of Christ (for believers) or punished at the Great White Throne Judgment (for non-believers). The Judgment Seat of Christ is mentioned in Romans 14:10-12 and applies to Christians only:

> **ROMANS 14: 10-12**
> *But why do you judge your brother? Or why do you show contempt for your brother? For we shall all stand before the judgment seat of Christ. For it is written: 'As I live, says the Lord, Every knee shall bow to Me, And every tongue*

shall confess to God.' So then each of us shall give account of himself to God.' At the Judgment Seat of Christ, believers will give an account of their lives to Christ. Believers are rewarded based on how they lived their lives and will receive crowns accordingly; 2 Timothy 2:5, 2 Timothy 4:8, James 1:12, 1 Peter 5:4, and Revelation 2:10. James 1:12 says that there is a reward as to how well we handle trials:

JAMES 1:12
Blessed is the man who perseveres under trial, because when he has stood the test, he will receive the crown of life that God has promised to those who love him.

The Great White Throne Judgment is mentioned in Revelation 20:11-15 and is the final judgment of non-believers before being cast into the lake of fire.

REVELATION 20:11-15
Then I saw a great white throne and Him who sat on it, from whose face the earth and the heaven fled away. And there was found no place for them. And I saw the dead, small and great, standing before God, and books were opened. And another book was opened, which is the Book of Life. And the dead were judged according to their works, by the things which were written in the books. The sea gave up the dead who were in it, and Death and Hades delivered up the dead who were in them. And they were judged, each one according to his works. Then Death and Hades were cast into the lake of fire. This is the second death. And anyone not found written in the Book of Life was cast into the lake of fire.

This event occurs after the millennium Kingdom and after Satan, the beast, and the false prophet are thrown into the lake of fire (Revelation 20:7-10). Books are opened (Revelation 20:12) containing records of everyone's deeds, whether good or evil, and will be judged accordingly (Romans 2:6). Regardless of why, regardless of influence, if you did it, you will have to give an account. Every single act will one day be examined by Jesus Christ as you stand in front of Him. Actually, we will give an account of every idle word we speak, Matthew 12:36 *"But I say unto you, That every idle word that men shall speak, they shall give account thereof in the day of judgment."* Since we are all going to give an account of our lives, we should choose carefully what we do and what we say--every act and every spoken word matters.

THE CAUSE OF MALADAPTIVE (EXTREME) BEHAVIOR

Since behavior is a choice as established from the Scripture, it is irresponsible to suggest that a person is not accountable for their behavior--even extreme, bizarre behavior.

Maladaptive and extreme behavior is the result of people not controlling their mind (thinking), emotions (feelings), or their will (choices). When a person fails to control their thoughts, they think too much about the wrong thing, which easily leads to depression. When people fail to control their emotions, they get angry and easily have outbursts. When people fail to control their will, they easily make poor choices.

The more out of control a person is over their mind, emotion, and will, the more likely they will have extreme behavior that will sanction a diagnostic label from the Psychiatric community.

SUMMARY

The Bible views behavior as a choice. The Scripture does not allow for an individual's behavior to be explained or excused any other way. We all inherited the sin nature from Adam and therefore do not want to do what God says. Because we have a sin nature, we get defensive when confronted with our rebellious choices, we fail to take responsibility for our choices, and we rationalize or blame someone or something for our choices.

The Holy Spirit works in our heart to influence us to obey Scripture, but Satan can influence us through temptation to disobey Scripture. People can influence us either positively or negatively. Regardless of the source of the influence every person is still responsible for the choices they make both good and bad. Our choices have consequences. Extreme behavior is explained by a lack of self-control.

We need to look no further than the Bible to explain all behavior. God holds everyone responsible for the choices they make and everyone will have to give an account for their life before Jesus Christ.

eleven

THE TEMPERAMENT MODEL OF BEHAVIOR

People are born with natural tendencies as discussed in my book, *The Temperament Model of Behavior: Understanding Your Natural Tendencies.* The Biblical view of maladaptive or extreme behavior is that such behavior is caused by a lack of self-control. Understanding that people are born with natural tendencies gives insight into what people naturally struggle with the most. As we will see, some people naturally struggle with being too aggressive, or too emotional, or being too stubborn, or being too analytical. When these natural tendencies (and others) are not controlled, it can lead to issues that will interfere with a person's life, sometimes severely. What the psychiatric community labels as a diagnosis is actually nothing more than a natural tendency that is out of control. Here is a brief description of the four temperaments.

CHOLERIC | The Choleric is extroverted, hot-tempered, quick thinking, active, practical, strong-willed, easily annoyed, and result-oriented. The Choleric has a huge ego, a firm expression, and is self-confident, self-sufficient, and very independent minded. They are decisive, opinionated and find it easy to make decisions for themselves as well as others.

SANGUINE | The Sanguine is extroverted, emotional, impulsive, fun-loving, activity-prone, entertaining, persuasive, easily amused, optimistic, and people-oriented. The Sanguine tends to be competitive, impulsive, and disorganized. The voice of the Sanguine will show excitement and friendliness. They have a natural smile and talk easily and often. They are animated, excitable, and accepting of others. They build relationships quickly and have lots of friends.

PHLEGMATIC | The Phlegmatic is introverted, calm, unemotional, slow moving, easygoing, accommodating, and service-oriented. The Phlegmatic does not show much emotion and will have a stoic expression. They are slow to warm up and indirect when interacting with others. The Phlegmatic lives a quiet, peaceful, routine life, free of the normal anxieties of the other temperaments. They avoid conflict and getting too involved with people and life.

MELANCHOLY | The Melancholy is introverted, logical, analytical, factual, private, conscientious, timid, and quality-oriented. The Melancholy will (most always) have a serious expression. They usually respond to others in a slow, cautious, and indirect manner. They are self-sacrificing, creative, and can be perfectionists. The Melancholy has high standards to avoid mistakes.

We are all a combination of the four temperaments, but we have one that is primary and one that is secondary. There are twelve blends, each combination comes with strengths and weaknesses. For more information, see the book mentioned above.

UNCONTROLLED TENDENCIES

Here are typical natural tendencies that, when not controlled, will cause any individual difficulty within themselves and with their relationships.

THE CHOLERIC | HIGH D
The Choleric (High D) is naturally result oriented. When they fail to get quick results they will show their frustration with explosive and demanding behavior that is intimidating. They will then try to control everyone and everything.

THE SANGUINE | HIGH I
The Sanguine (High I) is naturally people oriented. When they are rejected or embarrassed, they get verbally and even physically aggressive. They can talk and play too much.

THE PHLEGMATIC| HIGH S
The Phlegmatic (High S) is naturally accommodating. When they are faced with change (especially sudden change), they get extremely

stubborn and refuse to cooperate.

THE MELANCHOLY | HIGH C
The Melancholy (High C) likes to do things right and have a plan. They feel guilty when they cannot meet their own high standards. They react negatively when they have to change their plan without a logical reason and may withdraw. They think too much about the wrong thing causing sad and discouraged feelings.

ANXIETY, DEPRESSION AND BIPOLAR DISORDER EXPLAINED

When a person chooses not to obey Scripture and they fail to exercise self-control over their natural tendencies, they cause themselves difficulties, sometimes great difficulties. Here are some examples of why people naturally get anxious, depressed or have mood shifts.

ANXIETY

THE CHOLERIC | HIGH D
The Choleric will get anxious about not getting results fast enough or because people will not immediately do what they tell them to do.

THE SANGUINE | HIGH I
The Sanguine will get anxious about whether or not they are being respected by others. They get anxious if they think they are going to look bad in the eyes of others or they may be embarrassed or rejected.

THE PHLEGMATIC | HIGH S
The Phlegmatic gets anxious about having to change their routine or they are concerned that they may not be accommodating. They also get anxious if their home life is infringed upon.

THE MELANCHOLY | HIGH C
The Melancholy will get anxious if they do not have a plan in which to operate. They get anxious if they think they may be wrong. They also get anxious if they are around people too much.

People who get anxious are choosing to disobey Philippians 4:6-7 (see pages 24-26) and opens the door to allow their natural tendencies to control them instead of the Spirit of God. When a Christian feels anxiety, a choice is made to ignore God's command to not be anxious by involving God with prayer. When you obey God's promise, He will give you peace and then He will guard your heart from being anxious about...anything. The Biblical answer to anxiety is to obey Philippians 4:6-7 and choose not to be anxious.

DEPRESSION

As discussed earlier, (see pages 29-33) everyone will have disappointing events during their life that will challenge their mental and emotional state of equilibrium. It is human to feel sadness and remorse when such events occur. There is a normal period of adjustment that it takes to regain our usual mental and emotional sense of well-being. However, when depression is the routine way of dealing with life's difficulties or there is an extended period of time of depression, then another explanation is necessary.

As discussed, the psychiatric community basically holds that the underlying cause of depression is a chemical imbalance in the brain. Their position is that the brain is defective and therefore the person is a victim of faulty brain chemistry and in need of medication to correct the malady.

The Biblical view of why people get depressed is found in Jonah's struggle with his mission to Nineveh and the Lord (see page 30). Jonah disapproved of how God dealt with the people of Nineveh. He wanted God to destroy them but they repented. Jonah became depressed because of what he was thinking.

Simply put, people disturb themselves as did Jonah. I have never dealt with anyone that reported symptoms of depression who was unable to identify an event that was causing their emotional pain. When I point out that they are thinking too much about the wrong thing, everyone immediately agrees.

The issue is not something that their brain is doing to them because of the lack of brain chemistry balance, it is because they are disturbing themselves by negative thinking. People get stuck and they do not have an effective coping skill to get beyond the disturbing event that has occurred.

When there is a catastrophic life changing event, there will be great sadness and deep feelings of loss. This is a normal human experience. People who have healthy coping skills however, recover from a disappointing life event in a reasonable amount of time without medication. People that battle depressive feelings frequently are not good at solving problems. The Biblical answer for those who are depressed is to accept that God is conforming them into His likeness (Romans 8:28-29) and think on those things in Philippians 4:8. Remember that God does not do anything *to* you, He does it *for* you.

BIPOLAR DISORDER

People who are labeled bipolar have a combination of two natural temperaments that are opposite and opposing. They have a primary temperament need to be with people and socialize and a secondary temperament need to be alone to think and plan (Sanguine-Melancholy or I/C). These two temperament needs are literally polar opposites. When these two needs are managed well...all is well. When these two needs are not managed well, shifts in their mood are noticeable...sometimes they have wide mood shifts.

The Sanguine-Melancholy (I-C) is emotionally sensitive, typically creative and they have a deep, intense fear of being rejected. When they are disrespected, rejected, put down or embarrassed, their natural response is to display instant and extreme emotions. The diagnostic label given to such a person is often bipolar. This label is given to those who fail to control their natural tendencies. *They do not have a chemical-imbalance problem, they have a self-control problem.* The psychiatric community wants us to believe that it is caused by faulty brain chemistry. It is not. As mentioned, there is not one piece of scientific evidence to prove such a claim.

After being around thousands of bipolar people and counseling hundreds, I have never found one that did not have the Sanguine-Melancholy temperament blend. Of course, not everyone that is Sanguine-Melancholy is a candidate for being tagged as bipolar, *only those who routinely fail to control their mind, emotions and will.* It is only the Sanguine-Melancholy (I-C) that is given the label of being bipolar (when out-of-control).

Understanding that these people have natural tendencies that, when not controlled, will have mood shifts--this places the responsibility on the individual to exercise self-control. They do not have a defective brain. Their brain is capable of producing a wide range of emotion out of which comes amazing creativity. The Biblical answer for those tagged with being bipolar is to exercise self-control.

SUMMARY

People are born with natural tendencies (temperament). The instructions in the Bible are given for our good and when we fail to obey God's commands, we allow our natural tendencies to control our thoughts, emotions, and will. When we fail to control our natural tendencies and don't obey God we naturally become anxious, depressed, or have shifts in our emotional state.

part four
THE SPIRITUAL LIFE

twelve

THE SPIRITUAL LIFE AND COUNSELING

What exactly does it mean to live the spiritual life and how does it relate to counseling?

WHAT IS THE SPIRITUAL LIFE?

Living the spiritual life is the voluntary practice of Biblical truth through the work of the Holy Spirit that produces Christ-like maturity. The spiritual life can be lived effectively only in the context of a Christian community where there is Biblical instruction, example, and encouragement.

THE SPIRITUAL LIFE AND COUNSELING

Living life God's way enables the Christian to see life's difficulties and challenges as coming from God for the purpose of being conformed into the image of His Son (Romans 8:28-29). Living the spiritual life enables you to live above the circumstances of life without outside intervention or the use of medication. God has provided instructions in the Bible to follow and has given us the Holy Spirit to strengthen us to deal with virtually every aspect of life regardless of what happens.

Christians get anxious, discouraged, angry, depressed, and even turn to medication for relief because they are not seeing their life's events as coming from God's gracious Hand. These Christians fail to obey God's clear direction that would prevent strong, negative reactions to the twists and turns of life.

WHAT IT DOES NOT MEAN

Living the spiritual life does not mean that you will be free of difficulties. It does not mean that you will be able to handle everything life throws at you without having an emotional response and a need for support.

WHAT IT DOES MEAN

Living the spiritual life does mean that you will grow in the grace and knowledge of Jesus Christ as you respond Biblically to the circumstances in your life. It does mean that as you grow, you will experience the calm delight produced by the Holy Spirit as you respond appropriately to God's Word.

Living the spiritual life means that you will not need medication to get you through the dilemmas of life. The use of medication does not fix anything in the brain and only distracts one from taking accountability for their behavior.

WHAT ABOUT COUNSELING?

When in need of outside intervention, a Christian should always seek a Christian counselor or pastor that will guide them in understanding what God says about their struggle and their responsibility from God's Word. You can also seek other Christians who are living a Godly life for direction and support.

Living the spiritual life is not easy, but God has promised to help and empower you through virtually anything that happens in your life. Turn to God's Word with an open heart to find what He would have you do in your current circumstances.

thirteen

WHY IS LIVING THE SPIRITUAL LIFE SO HARD?

Christian's seek counseling because they are overwhelmed with life's circumstances, they are having relationship problems, or they have been told they have a mental disorder. As I have said, there are other reasons but these are the most common I've encountered in my practice as a therapist.

As presented in this book, I believe that the answers Christian's seek to the problems they face are not found in psychiatry or psychology. God has given us His Word and it is here that we find the answers to every problem we have. God did not give us answers to many or even most problems, He has given us answers to *all* of our problems. Your task is to study God's Word, find out what to do... and do it. I know, you're thinking that's hard! That's close. Actually, it's impossible. As we are about to see, we need the Holy Spirit to work in our life and empower us to obey God's Word.

Every Christian can relate to the struggle of living the Christian life as Paul did:

ROMANS 7:15-24
For what I am doing, I do not understand. For what I will to do, that I do not practice; but what I hate, that I do. If, then, I do what I will not to do, I agree with the law that it is good. But now, it is no longer I who do it, but sin that dwells in me. For I know that in me (that is, in my flesh) nothing good dwells; for to will is present with me, but how to perform what is good I do not find. For the good that I will to do, I do not do; but the evil I will not to do, that I practice. Now if I do what I will not to do, it is no longer I who do it, but sin that dwells in me. I find then a law, that evil is present with me, the one who wills to do good. For I delight in the law of God according to the inward man. But I see another law in my members, warring against the law of my mind, and bringing me into captivity to the law of sin which is in my members. O wretched

man that I am! Who will deliver me from this body of death?

Becoming a Christian assured us of going to Heaven, but it did not rid us of the rebellious nature we inherited from Adam (Romans 5:12-21). It is this inherited, rebellious nature that causes us to struggle as Paul did with living the Spiritual life.

Thousands of years after Jeremiah wrote that the heart is deceitful (Jeremiah 17:9), James picks up on the same theme (James 1:22) and tells us that a Christian is deceived if they fail to do what God has said. It is not in the *knowing* that solves our problems, it is in the *doing* what God has said.

There is no hope for dealing with life's difficulties apart from knowing and doing what God has told us to do. Not doing what God said got us into this mess--Adam's sin. Doing what God said will get you out of the mess you are in. Charles Swindall said, "Wisdom occurs when knowledge produces obedience." It is not just about knowing, it is about doing.

SUMMARY

It is impossible to live the spiritual life without the help of the Holy Spirit because we inherited our rebellious hearts from Adam. We do not want to be accountable for our behavior so we get defensive, rationalize, and shift blame to someone or something else.

Living a spiritual life is about being conformed into His image so we will be like Him and not do these things. The responsibility of every Christian is to know what God said and apply it to their lives every day and in every situation.

fourteen

DESIRE

The process of living the spiritual life begins with your desire to grow spiritually. The following verses show that from the beginning God has asked us to respond to Him with a strong, unyielding desire to know Him. He wants to have a deep, personal relationship with you but He wants you to want it too.

WILL YOU FIGHT FOR IT?

Jacob wrestled with the Lord to get a blessing as recorded in Genesis 32:26, *"And He said, 'Let Me go, for the day breaks.' But he [Jacob]said, 'I will not let You go unless You bless me!'"* This is the kind of desire and tenacity that is necessary to grow spiritually.

We are surrounded by illustrations of people who accomplished something because of having a strong desire to do so. For example, those who get a college degree work hard over a long period of time, determined to reach their goal of graduation. Those who want a particular career, work hard to acquire the knowledge and skills to work in their chosen field. Those in sales are successful because of a strong desire to earn a living by selling their product. Whenever anyone accomplishes anything in life, it is the result of having a strong desire to do so and a determination to never give up. If you are going to grow spiritually, you must have that same, unyielding desire and never give up.

WILL YOU SEARCH FOR IT?

Everyone finds what they are looking for, *"He who earnestly seeks good finds favor, but trouble will come to him who seeks evil"* (Proverbs 11:27). The contrast in this proverb is between one seeking good and the other seeking evil. Both found what they were seeking.

WHAT AM I TO DESIRE?

There are four things a believer is to desire in order to grow spiritually:

THE LORD

The Psalmist compares his longing for The Lord to the desire a deer has for water.

> **PSALMS 42:1**
> *As the deer pants for the water brooks, so pants my soul for You, O God.*

The Psalmist longed more than anything else to know the Lord in a deeply personal way.

TO FOLLOW HIM

> **LUKE 9:23-26**
> *Then He said to them all, "If anyone desires to come after Me, let him deny himself, and take up his cross daily, and follow Me. For whoever desires to save his life will lose it, but whoever loses his life for My sake will save it. For what profit is it to a man if he gains the whole world, and is himself destroyed or lost? For whoever is ashamed of Me and My words, of him the Son of Man will be ashamed when He comes in His own glory, and in His Father's, and of the holy angels.*

Jesus gave us the requirements needed to follow Him. We are to say "No" to ourselves which includes pleasures or possessions. If we gain everything in this life but not the Lord then we have gained nothing. We are to take up our cross and follow the Lord which means to be identified with Him by surrendering, suffering, and sacrificing.

RIGHTEOUSNESS

Early in Jesus' ministry He delivered the Sermon on the Mount and said, *"Blessed are those who hunger and thirst for righteousness, For they shall be filled"* (Matthew 5:6).

To be blessed you have to hunger and thirst after righteousness. The word for "hunger" here means *a strong craving as if you are famished*. All of us have been hungry after going longer than we should to eat. Hunger is caused by waiting too long to eat. The longer you wait the more desperate you feel. All you think about is food, the kind doesn't matter, you just want food! In this state you really find it difficult to think about anything else...you just want something to eat! That kind of strong desire motivates you to seek and find food. Once you fill your stomach, you are temporarily satisfied until later...then you want more food. Jesus is saying that if you want to be really satisfied then hunger and thirst after righteousness. It is the only way to be truly satisfied.

THE WORD

Peter put it this way, *"Therefore, laying aside all malice, all deceit, hypocrisy, envy, and all evil speaking, as newborn babes, desire the pure milk of the word, that you may grow thereby"* (1 Peter 2:1-2).

The word translated "desire" means *to intensely crave the possession of something.* The inference is that Christians should want the Word just as intensely as a baby wants milk. It's the same strong desire that Jesus spoke about in Matthew 5:6 mentioned above.

IT TAKES ALL OF YOU

A person becomes a Christian when he or she trusts Jesus Christ for the gift of eternal life (John 3:16). After becoming a Christian the new believer is to be transformed into the image of Jesus Christ (Romans 8:28-29).

To say that becoming a mature Christian does not happen overnight is an understatement; it is a process that spans the life of every believer. Actually, the work is never completed on this earth. The good news is that a transformation does take place as you cooperate with the work of the Holy Spirit and strive to apply God's Word to your daily life. The key is involving God in your life's struggles and choosing to do what He has said. This requires reading and studying the Bible with the intent to practice what He has said.

To mature and have a strong desire for the Lord and to know the Scripture, you must be motivated. To be motivated you must involve your will, mind, and emotions.

WILL

You must first *decide* that you want to grow spiritually. That sounds elementary, but it is the most important and the most difficult step to take. You cannot say, "I would like to grow so I will try hard." To start with you are going to *try* hard is to give yourself an out. Your rational would then be, "Well, I did really *try!*" When a decision is *first* made to desire spiritual growth and to know the Scripture, you will then voluntarily take the next step.

MIND

You must then engage your thoughts on the Scripture. That includes not only reading the Bible but studying to find out what you need to do. Psalms 1:1-3 says you will be blessed if you delight in His Word:

> **PSALMS 1:1-3**
> **Blessed** *is the man who walks not in the counsel of the ungodly, Nor stands in the path of sinners, Nor sits in the seat of the scornful; But his* **delight** *is in the law of the Lord, And in His law he* **meditates** *day and night. He shall be like a tree planted by the rivers of water, that brings forth its fruit in its season, whose leaf also shall not wither; and whatever he does shall prosper.* [Emphasis added]

The Hebrew word for *blessed* is happy. The psalmist is saying happiness comes from delighting in God's Word and mediating on it day and night. To meditate means to think about what the Scripture means and how to apply it to your daily life. As a student at Dallas Theological Seminary, I heard Dr. Howard Hendricks say many times, "Gentlemen, always have something on your back burner!" He was encouraging us to have a passage of Scripture ready to think about when we have a moment to ourselves.

EMOTIONS

After you decide to know the Scripture and begin filling your mind with His truth, you will experience emotions of joy, peace and praise. You will get excited when you begin to discover truth on your own and you will want to know more.

Psalms 146: 1-10 was written to praise God because the writer had seen God work and he could not contain his excitement:

> **PSALMS 146:1-10**
> *Praise the Lord!*
> *Praise the Lord, O my soul!*
> *While I live I will praise the Lord;*
> *I will sing praises to my God while I have my being.*
> *Do not put your trust in princes,*

Nor in a son of man, in whom there is no help.
His spirit departs, he returns to his earth;
In that very day his plans perish.
Happy is he who has the God of Jacob for his help,
Whose hope is in the Lord his God,
Who made heaven and earth,
The sea, and all that is in them;
Who keeps truth forever,
Who executes justice for the oppressed,
Who gives food to the hungry.
The Lord gives freedom to the prisoners.
The Lord opens the eyes of the blind;
The Lord raises those who are bowed down;
The Lord loves the righteous.
The Lord watches over the strangers;
He relieves the fatherless and widow;
But the way of the wicked He turns upside down.
The Lord shall reign forever—
Your God, O Zion, to all generations.
Praise the Lord!

SUMMARY

Desire is the starting place for the believer to live the Spiritual life. Remember, Jesus said that we must hunger and thirst after righteousness and if you do, you will be satisfied (Matthew 5:6). God will not fill your cup until you take off the lid. You have to open your heart and be willing.

fifteen

VOLUNTARILY OBEY

Having the desire to grow spiritually is the necessary first step. Desire must then be followed by volunteering yourself (Romans 12:1) to the process of being transformed. To desire to know Him and the power of His resurrection (Philippians 3:10) is to be willing to voluntarily submit yourself to God and obey His Word.

I BESEECH YOU

ROMANS 12:1
I beseech you therefore, brethren, by the mercies of God, that you present your bodies a living sacrifice, holy, acceptable to God, which is your reasonable service.

In this passage, the "therefore" is a response to what Paul says in Romans 5:1 and Romans 6:13,16 that we are justified by faith and we are to obey God. Paul is now asking believers to do something based on what he has previously said. He begins by writing "I beseech you" (Romans 12:1). The word translated as "beseech" holds the idea of *to invite*, so it's an invitation rather than a command. Paul is strongly encouraging his readers to voluntarily do three things; present their bodies as a living sacrifice (Romans 12:1), to not be conformed to this world (Romans 12:2), and that their minds be renewed (Romans 12:2).

What a shocking word is used in Romans 12:1, "beseech" The God of creation against Whom we all stand guilty of sin. The God Who provided salvation through the sacrifice of His Son. The all powerful, all knowing, all present God of this universe said, "I *beseech* you!" Wow! God is *asking* you, *not commanding* you, to respond based on what He has done for you. How can any believer not respond to such love?

Paul's argument in Romans 12:1 is that it is *reasonable* to present our bodies (our whole being including mind, emotions, and will) to God as a living sacrifice. The Greek word here translated *reasonable* means *logical*. Paul makes it clear that it is a logical conclusion to voluntarily give yourself to God because you have been justified by faith.

SUMMARY

Living the Spiritual life begins with a desire to do so. Your desire must then be proven by actually volunteering yourself to God as a living sacrifice (Romans 12:1). Since living the Spiritual life is not a command, God will not force you against your will. He wants you to want it. He appeals to believers based on what He has already done and asks us to walk worthy of His calling (Ephesians 4:1-7).

Over 300 years ago Isaac Watts thought about the sacrifice that Jesus made on the cross and he was stunned and overwhelmed with the debt he could never repay. Review the words on the next page.

WHEN I SURVEY THE WONDROUS CROSS

When I survey the wondrous cross
On which the Prince of glory died,
My richest gain I count but loss,
And pour contempt on all my pride.

Forbid it, Lord, that I should boast,
Save in the death of Christ my God!
All the vain things that charm me most,
I sacrifice them to His blood.

See from His head, His hands, His feet,
Sorrow and love flow mingled down!
Did e'er such love and sorrow meet,
Or thorns compose so rich a crown?

Were the whole realm of nature mine,
That were a present far too small;
Love so amazing, so divine,
Demands my soul, my life, my all.

-Isaac Watts, 1707

sixteen

DO NOT BE CONFORMED TO THIS WORLD

Paul's appeal to his readers continues in Romans 12:2 but now he tells them... *"do not be conformed to this world..."* What does it mean to not be conformed to this world? Does Paul mean to do as the Monks do and withdraw from society to study the Bible and pray? Does Paul mean to do as the Amish and refuse to use modern technology and conveniences such as electricity? If this is what Paul means then the Gospel would not have been spread by the early Christians; they would have been too busy studying and praying to talk to others. Furthermore the writers of the New Testament would have written about the worldly use of boats and nets to catch fish if using modern day tools was sinful. To gain a clear understanding of what Paul is saying we need to investigate two words; *conformed* and *world*.

CONFORMED

In Romans 8:29 Paul said that we are to be *conformed* into the "image of His Son." The word "conformed" here means *to have the same form as another*. Christians are to have the same form as Jesus Christ; He was full of grace and truth (John 1:14). They are to think as He did and behave as He did.

In Romans 12:2 Paul says we are not to be conformed to this world. He uses a different word for *conformed* here which means to be "similar in character." Christians are not to have the same character as the world. The contrast is clear. We are to be *conformed* to Christ's image and not be *conformed* to the world's image.

WORLD

In Romans 12:2 Paul said that we are not to be conformed to this *world*. The term "world" (*kosmos*) in the New Testament is used in three ways. Sometimes it refers to the *physical* world (Hebrews 1:10). Sometimes it refers to the world of *people* (John 3:16), and other times it refers to *world system* as ruled by Satan (John 12:31).

Here in Romans 12:2 Paul uses a different word for *world (aion)* which means *age* or *present time*. The Greek word *aion* is, by implication, referring to the world system but a specific period of time of the world system; specifically the time in which you are now living. So Paul is saying that Christians are not to be like the present age in which they are living.

Two of the passages that write about being associated with the world system as ruled by Satan are James 4:1-10 and 1 John 2:15-17. These two passages represent the beginning and the end of the New Testament writings; James was the first book written between 45-50 A.D. and 1 John was one of the last books written between 85-97 A.D.. The issue of being conformed to the world was addressed for a span of roughly fifty years...and is still needed today.

BEFRIENDING THE WORLD

JAMES 4:1-4
Where do wars and fights come from among you? Do they not come from your desires for pleasure that war in your members? You lust and do not have. You murder and covet and cannot obtain. You fight and war. Yet you do not have because you do not ask. You ask and do not receive, because you ask amiss, that you may spend it on your pleasures. Adulterers and adulteresses! Do you not know that friendship with the world is enmity with God? Whoever therefore wants to be a friend of the world makes himself an enemy of God.

To have your selfish desires lead to fighting with others is to be like the world (James 4:1). Fighting is what happens when you leave God out of your life and try to do it your way. James then tells his readers that they do not have because they do not ask God (James 4:2) and when they do ask it is for selfish reasons (James 4:3). James has harsh words for his readers by saying that their selfishness left God out and fighting causes them to become a friend of the world and an enemy of God (James 4:4). The word "friend" means *fond of* and the word "enemy" means *to be hostile toward* someone; which in this verse is God. When you are being so selfish that you are fighting with others, you're being fond of the world and hostile toward God.

ALL THAT IS IN THE WORLD

1 JOHN 2:15-16
Do not love the world or the things in the world. If anyone loves the world, the love of the Father is not in him. For all that is in the world; the lust of the flesh, the lust of the eyes, and the pride of life; is not of the Father but is of the world.

The Apostle John wrote toward the end of his life to encourage his readers to avoid involvement in the world system over which Satan is the ruler. Here's my brother Mike's treatment of 1 John 2:15-16 (Dr. Mike Cocoris, The Spiritual Life, Clarifying The Confusion, page 73):

> The phrase 'the love of the Father' means love for the father. By saying 'love for the Father' instead of 'love for God,' John is pointing to the duty of the believers as children of God. If believers love the world, the love for the Father is not in them as the controlling factor in their life. To love the world is to venerate and value, cherish and choose that which is opposite to God.
>
> John identifies the individual components of the world. First is the *lust of the flesh*. The Greek word rendered 'lust' means 'desire,' not necessarily sexual desire, just desire. When it is the lust of the flesh it probably refers to a desire for sinful (probably sensual) pleasure, especially sexual pleasure. The *lust of the eye* consists of desires that come through, or are motivated by the eye. In other words, it is the desire to have what one sees. The thought is covetousness and greed aroused by what is seen. The last is the *pride of life*. The Greek word rendered 'life' is not the normal word for life in the New Testament. This one means 'period of life, course of life, livelihood.' It refers to the means by which life is sustained. Thus, 'the pride of life' refers to a proud, boastful, arrogant attitude concerning one's possessions or position, station or status. All three phrases describe the lifestyle that is opposite to and is opposed to God.
>
> In a sense, the world wants pleasure, possessions, and power. The various world systems, the political world, the business world, the sports world, the religious world are about pleasure, possessions, and power apart from God. Those are the enemies of the spiritual life, because if you live for those things, you will not be walking with the Lord. People of the world seek pleasures that have diminishing returns. Each experience becomes less and less thrilling. It requires more to

produce the same effect. Such pleasures are like a drug, which becomes less and less effective. How foolish to seek pleasure in things that offer diminishing returns. People of the world seek possessions that wear out like a pair of shoes. Poet Robert Burns wrote:

"Pleasures are like poppies spread
You seize the flower, its bloom is shed
Or like the snow falls in the river,
A moment white—then melts forever"

According to these two passages (James 4:1-4 and 1 John 2:15-16), being conformed to this world or being a friend to this world includes such things as being selfish to the point of conflict, having inappropriate sexual desires, being greedy, or being boastful about your possessions or position in life. This is how the world thinks and behaves and when a Christian does these things, John says you cannot have love *for* the Father (1 John 2:15). Anything that leaves the Lord out of your life is conformity to the world system.

DEMAS

Demas was Paul's companion and was with him during his first imprisonment. He was heavily involved in ministry and was deeply committed or he would not have been with Paul in Rome. Paul wrote his letter to the Christians in Colossae 20 years after the book of James was written (approximately 67 A.D.) and sent greetings to them from Luke and Demas (Colossians 4:14). Paul sadly wrote later in 2 Timothy 4:10 *"for Demas has forsaken me, having loved this present world, and has departed for Thessalonica—Crescens for Galatia, Titus for Dalmatia."*

Demas apparently valued what the world offered to the point that he abandoned Paul in his time of need making him an example of what not to do. He was with Paul but his heart was in the world, so it's possible to even be in the ministry and your heart be somewhere else. What distracted Demas is not revealed, just that the things of the world were more important than serving the Lord by helping Paul. According to Solomon, "There is nothing new under the sun" (Ecclesiastes 1:9) so we do not have to strain to figure out what may have drawn Demas away. The list would include the usual suspects like money, possessions, power, or pleasure. These things do not have to be a problem but if these (or anything else) leaves God out then they qualify for being called the things of this world.

SUMMARY

Being a friend of the world (being conformed to the world) is a choice you make to leave God out. Being a friend of the world is to act like people who do not know the Lord as Savior.

seventeen

RENEW YOUR MIND

To not be conformed to the world's way of thinking and behaving requires a change of mind. Notice Romans 12:2, "...*but be transformed by the renewing of your mind, that you may prove what is that good and acceptable and perfect will of God.*" The Greek word translated as "renewing" means to *renovate*. When you renovate something you remove the *old* and replace it with the *new*. A room can be renovated or the whole house, it depends on the condition of the house. When the renovation has been completed the room has changed from what it was (the old) to what it is (the new). During the *renovation*, changes in the room are noticeable to one observing.

We cannot grow spiritually without changing our thinking. God uses trials to get our attention so we can align our thinking to His way of thinking. To grow spiritually you have to align your thinking to what God says about issues like the ones we have discussed; trials, getting anxious, relationship difficulties, and self control.

TRIALS

As covered in Chapters 1-5, God doesn't do anything *to* us, he does it *for* us to conform us into the image of His Son (Romans 8:28-29). Adjust your thinking and emotions to this truth when a trial occurs and you will grow spiritually.

ANXIETY

As covered in Chapter 4, Paul told the believers in Philippi not to be anxious. Instead, involve God in what you are concerned about by praying and giving thanks. When something happens that you do not like, choose to not be anxious. If you remember this truth, adjust your thinking and emotions *and* choose not become anxious, you will grow spiritually.

RELATIONSHIPS

As covered in Chapter 6-7, we are to treat people as God treats us. Practice loving people, forgiving people and showing grace to people. Adjust your thinking and emotions when you have friction with someone and treat them as God treats you and you will grow spiritually.

MENTAL DISORDERS

As covered in Chapters 8-11, a mental disorder label is given to people who fail to exercise self-control. Control what you think, feel and do and you will have inward peace and grow spiritually

RENOVATE YOUR THINKING

Paul's appeal to Christians to renovate (change) their thinking and behavior is based on the work that God has done for every believer. In Romans he said we are justified by faith (Romans 5:1). In Ephesians Paul reminded us that we are chosen, adopted, accepted, redeemed and sealed by the Holy Spirit (Ephesians 1:3-13). In Colossians 3:1, Paul says we are risen with Christ. Based on these incomprehensible truths, Paul says volunteer yourself to God (Romans 12:1), walk worthy of what God has done fore you (Ephesians 4:1) for this is only reasonable (Romans 12:1).

Every Christian ought to be involved in the process of renovating (changing) their way of thinking and behaving (see the lists in Ephesians 4:22-32 and Colossians 3:5-25). Let's see how the process of renovating your mind works by referring to verses previously mentioned. Here are some things to stop doing and new things to start doing:

WHAT TO STOP

1. STOP REACTING TO WHAT PEOPLE SAY AND DO TO YOU

1 Corinthians 13:4 says that love is patient which means that love never takes the opportunity to avenge itself. Love absorbs offenses, criticism, and slander for the sake of others. Love doesn't get defensive, rationalize accountability, or shift blame to avoid responsibility. Jesus absorbed all that was done to Him and He is our example to follow. Don't react...***absorb***. Don't strike back...***absorb***. Do not get defensive and react...***absorb***. Do not blame shift...***absorb***.

I counseled one gentleman that had a strong personality and would often and quickly show strong emotion when displeased (especially with his wife). I encouraged him to change the way he was thinking and pointed out that according to 1 Corinthians 13:4-8, love does not get irritated and is kind. He realized that he became upset because he did not do what God said, so he began working diligently to avoid saying what he was thinking and feeling. This was a great step forward in his maturing process. He changed (renovated) his thinking and learned to control his emotions.

Put off what you used to do and put on this new way of responding to people. When you are offended...stop, absorb, and do not react. Choose to respond in love and the Holy Spirit will be there to empower you. Remember when people say and do unkind things to you, God will use it to conform you into the image of His Son (Romans 8:28-29).

2. STOP SAYING UNKIND THINGS ABOUT/TO PEOPLE

1 Corinthians 13:4 says that love is kind which means that love never offends, insults or says anything unkind. Love is gracious and says gracious things that build up and does not tear down (Ephesians 4:32). If you can't say anything nice and uplifting, then don't say anything.

Proverbs 10:19 warns the one who talks a lot, *"You will say the wrong thing if you talk too much--so be sensible and watch what you say"* (CEV). Form the habit of saying encouraging things. Watch your tone of voice so that it does not communicate a negative edge. Do not use sarcastic humor.

Put off what you used to do and put on this new way of responding to people. When you are tempted to say something unkind...stop and **absorb.** Choose to respond in love and the Holy Spirit will be there to empower you. Remember when people insult you, God will use the event to conform you into the image of His Son.

3. STOP GETTING IRRITATED WITH PEOPLE

1 Corinthians 13:5 says that love is *not provoked* which means that love does not get irritated (this is not a misprint). God really means that believers are not to get irritated about anything at anytime. Righteous indignation not included; see Psalms 7:11, 1 Kings 11:9-10, and John 2:13-16.

Ever been cut off in traffic? Ever have a sales person be less than nice to you? Someone ever snap at you? Stop getting irritated when your mate, friend, relative, or stranger says or does something that bothers you.

Put off what you used to do and put on this new way of responding to people. When you have the opportunity to get irritated with someone...stop and **absorb.** Choose to respond in love and the Holy Spirit will be there to empower you. Remember when people do things that irritate you, it is being used to conform you into the image of His Son.

4. STOP REMINDING PEOPLE OF THEIR PAST MISTAKES

1 Corinthians 13:5 says that love thinks no evil, which means that love does not keep account of evil deeds, it forgives. Sorry, not a misprint here either. Believers are not allowed to bring up past sins! When couples come in for counseling it is always because they are beating each other up over what has happened in the past. You are not to bring up the past of others because God doesn't bring up your past (Hebrews 8:12). Actually He cannot do that because you are forgiven and you are to forgive others because of that (Ephesians 4:32). Psalms 103:12 tells us that He has separated us from our sins as far as the East is from the West.

Put off what you used to do and put on this new way of responding to people. When you are tempted to remind someone of their past mistakes...stop and absorb. Choose to respond in love and the Holy Spirit will be there to empower you. When others bring up your past mistakes, do not react or get irritated. Respond in love because it is being used to conform you into the image of His Son.

5. STOP ARGUING

This is one of the most difficult Biblical truths to get Christians to see. It is almost always the root cause of a diminished relationship. People argue because they want to be right, to defend themselves, and/or maintain control in the relationship. Arguing is not allowed according to Proverbs 17:14 which says, *"Starting a quarrel is like breaching a dam; so drop the matter before a dispute breaks out"* (NIV).

I saw a couple that had argued so much over one incident that it caused a major meltdown of their relationship. To say they were both angry would not be an adequate description, they were seething! They asked for an emergency meeting to discuss their disagreement. They both came with sufficient evidence to prove their point and they both were convinced that I would side with them once I heard their facts.

The husband was first and talked for 45 minutes non-stop. When it was my turn to talk...I said simply, that what he had just explained to me with deep emotion was *not* the problem. They both looked at me like I was the one in need of counseling. I said the problem is that this *became a problem* and that's the problem. It should have never been a problem in the first place! I said, "the Bible does not allow us to argue and you've been arguing about this for over a day."

Neither one were right, they were both wrong because they argued! We are not allowed to argue, we are to ***absorb*** and not strike back. Remember, what you argue about is not really the problem, *that* you argue *is* the problem. So do not argue...***absorb.*** Deal with it so it does not linger--let it go.

Put off what you used to do and put on this new way of responding to people. When you are faced with an opportunity to argue...stop and ***absorb.*** Choose to respond in love and the Holy Spirit will be there to empower you. Respond in love because it is being used to conform you into the image of His Son.

6. STOP BEING ANXIOUS

When you fail to involve God in whatever is going on in your life, you become anxious. Some pray about their situation but keep the anxiety. Sorry, but you can't do that. God said not to be anxious (Philippians 4:6-7), *"Be anxious for nothing, but by prayer and supplication, let your requests be known unto God."* When you take everything away from something, you have nothing left. That's what you are to be anxious for...nothing! Do not be concerned because He is in control and whatever He does is best for you and it will conform you into the image of His Son.

Stop what you used to do and *start* this new way of responding to life. Choose not to be anxious and the Holy Spirit will be there to empower you. When you are faced with the opportunity to become anxious...stop and give it to the Lord. He is using this issue to conform you into the image of His son.

7. STOP HANGING ON TO HURT...LET IT GO

When we are disrespected, insulted or criticized, we hang on to the hurt feelings-- damaging important relationships. 1 Corinthians 12:4-8 teaches us to not get irritated or offended and to not hold on to the past. That includes what happened a second ago. Let it go! Leave it in the past!

Put off what you used to do and put on this new way of responding to insults and criticisms. Choose to respond in love and the Holy Spirit will be there to empower you. When you are faced with the opportunity to react...stop and absorb. Respond in love because it is being used to conform you into the image of His Son.

WHAT TO START

1. START DOING

When I point out to believers in counseling what God said they should do, like practice 1 Corinthians 13:4-8, they look at me like that thought never occurred to them. They are living their lives the way they want to even though it is not working well. The focus of the Bible is *not* on fixing other people so they will stop doing things to you. The focus of the Bible is for you to respond Biblically to what is happening in your life so God can conform you into the image of His Son. That's why James said *"But be ye doers of the Word, and not hearers only, deceiving your own selves"* (James 1:22).

The only way to grow spiritually is to meditate on the Word of God so you can put it into practice. Psalms 1:1-2 states *"Blessed is the man that walketh not in the counsel of the ungodly...and in His law doth he meditate day and night."*

The clear message of Scripture is on *you* and *your* responsibility to obey His Word. God does not hold you responsible for others being conformed into His image, He holds you responsible for *you* and *you* only.

Put off what you used to do and put on this new way of responding to life. Choose to study the Bible and the Holy Spirit will be there to enlighten and empower you. Study to discover how God wants you to behave. As you *do* the Word of God, He will conform you into the image of His Son.

God blesses His Word. Therefore, spiritual growth occurs when you do what God said *because* God said it. The idea is this; "I am not going to get irritated because God said not to in 1 Corinthians 13:5. I will not argue because God said not to in Proverbs 17:14. I will not be anxious because God said not to be in Philippians 4:6-7."

2. START TRUSTING

Many Christians often fall apart emotionally when trials rush into their lives. However, trials are God's chosen method of transforming us into the image of His Son. Do as Proverbs 3:5-6 tells us to do:

> **PROVERBS 3:5-6**
> *Trust in the LORD with all your heart, and lean not on your own understanding; in all your ways acknowledge Him, and He shall direct your paths.*

Realize that God loves you and wants you to be like Him. Trust Him that He knows what is best for you even in your present circumstances.

Put off what you used to think and put on this new way of responding to life. Accept your circumstances as coming from God to conform you into the image of His Son.

3. START LETTING GOD TRANSFORM YOU

God wants to transform you into the image of His Son (Romans 8:28-29). He does this by bringing trials into your life and He wants you to respond Biblically. Let God do His work in you, don't give up. Paul reminded us in Galatians 6:9:

GALATIANS 6:9
And let us not grow weary while doing good, for in due season we shall reap if we do not lose heart.

God loves you and knows what's best for you. Cooperate with the work of the Holy Spirit in your life by learning Biblical principles and applying them to your life daily. Renovate (change) your thinking by putting off the old way of thinking and putting on the new way of thinking. As you do, He will transform you into the image of His Son.

HOW TO MEASURE GROWTH

A person's temperature is measured by a thermometer. Spiritual growth is measured by *how long it takes you to respond Biblically to a painful or disturbing event.*

God allows us some time to adjust or else He would not have said in Ephesians 4:26 *"Be angry, and do not sin, do not let the sun go down on your wrath."* Even in the case of such a strong emotion as anger He gave us a short amount of time to deal with it and move on. The Scripture is absent of directives that allow for an extended amount of time to get over a painful event. God requires believers to accept the event and move on with their lives.

It is an issue of spiritual maturity when a Christian holds on to their pain beyond a reasonable amount of time to adjust. There is no set time that applies to everyone because people handle emotional pain differently.

Thinking Biblically, we are to forgive others for the wrong done to us and let it go. Not years later...but now. So, when someone says that they need time to heal over their past they are really saying that they are not ready to understand, agree and do what God has said.

BE WILLING TO ADJUST

Look at King David's response to the death of his baby as recorded in 2 Samuel 12:15-23. David first pleaded with God to spare the life of his newborn baby (2 Samuel 12:16-17). When David heard his servants whispering he knew that the baby had died. Once he confirmed that it was so, he got up, cleaned up, worshiped the Lord and then ate (2 Samuel 12:20). This was so shocking to his servants that they marveled at his sudden emotional reversal (2 Samuel 12:21).

David had asked God to spare the baby's life. Now that God had taken the baby to Heaven, there was no longer a need for prayer and fasting (2 Samuel 12:23). David said that he would go to him but the baby would not return to him. David immediately adjusted because he accepted God's will. By the way, that is the only passage in the Bible that tells us that a baby goes to heaven.

BE WILLING TO LEARN

We all have a learning process to go through if we are to grow spiritually. It is painful but necessary to experience God's trials to become like His Son. Jesus said in Matthew 11:29 *"Take my yoke upon you and learn from Me, for I am gentle and lowly in heart, and you will find rest for your souls."* We are to take His yoke and learn from Him how to be humble. In Philippians 4:11 Paul wrote *"Not that I speak in regard to need, for I have learned in whatever state I am, to be content."* Paul had to learn what Jesus said. He did and had peace no matter what he experienced.

BE WILLING TO ACCEPT SUFFERING

In order to grow spiritually, we will suffer as the Lord did. 1 Peter 2:21 states *"For to this you were called, because Christ also suffered for us, leaving us an example, that you should follow His steps."*

How did the Lord suffer? He was *betrayed* by Judas (Matthew 26:14-16), *denied* by Peter (Matthew 26:69-75), and *abandoned* by his disciples (Matthew 26:56). While He was here He was *misunderstood, misrepresented, mistreated* and then He was *crucified!* Jesus has been through it all and understands our pain (Hebrews 2:18).

As you journey through this life you too may be betrayed, denied, and abandoned by someone close. You may experience being misunderstood, misrepresented, and mistreated by others. When one or more of these things happen to you, remember you are being conformed into the image of His Son (Romans 8:28-29) and you are sharing in His suffering (1 Peter 2:21). Do not take it personally, as if it is unfair, it is a privilege and an honor to suffer like He did. Renovate (change) your thinking to view these moments as coming from God to conform you into His image.

SUMMARY

In order to grow spiritually, you must renovate (change) your thinking by putting off your old way of thinking and putting on a new way of thinking. This includes what you think about trials in your life, what you think when you become anxious over a concern, and what you do when there is friction with someone else.

It may also include what you may have thought about having a mental disorder. The renovating process includes, but is not limited to the following: stop reacting to what people say and do to you; stop saying unkind things to people; stop getting irritated with people; stop reminding people of their past mistakes; let the past go; start doing; start trusting; and let God transform you.

You can track your spiritual growth by measuring how long it takes you to adjust Biblically to a painful moment or disturbing event.

eighteen

DEPEND ON THE HOLY SPIRIT

We are to renovate (renew) our mind by putting off the old and putting on the new (Ephesians 4:21-32 and Colossians 3:1-25). But we cannot do this under our own power. Actually, we are told that we can do nothing without Him (John 15:5) *"I am the vine, you are the branches. He who abides in Me, and I in him, bears much fruit; for without Me you can do nothing."* Jesus said He would leave behind a "helper" (John 14:16-17). The Holy Spirit helps us then by teaching us and reminding us of Scripture:

JOHN 14:26
But the Helper, the Holy Spirit, whom the Father will send in My name, He will teach you all things, and bring to your remembrance all things that I said to you.

You cannot do the Word as James directs (James 1:22) without the Holy Spirit empowering you to obey. As you involve yourself in doing what God has said to do in His Word, you are *"strengthened with might through the Spirit in the inner man"* (Ephesians 3:16). As the Holy Spirit works in you He produces the fruit of the Spirit (Galatians 5:22-23).

In *The Spiritual Life, Clarifying The Confusion*, Dr. Mike Cocoris goes over how to cooperate with the working of the Holy Spirit (pages 47-48):

DEAL WITH SIN
Paul says, *"Do not grieve the Holy Spirit of God, by whom you were sealed for the day of redemption"* (Eph. 4:30). What grieves the Holy Spirit? In a word—sin.

DO THE WILL OF GOD
Paul commands, *"Do not quench the Spirit"* (1 Thess. 5:19). The word

"quench" means *to extinguish, to put out*. It was used of putting out a fire. The Spirit, here, refers to the activity of the Spirit or the operation of the gifts of the Spirit. In other words, Paul is saying, "Do not prohibit the free exercise of spiritual gifts in the assembly." We quench the Holy Spirit when we do not do the will of God. So in essence this is saying, "Do the will of God."

DEPEND ON THE HOLY SPIRIT
Paul says, *"Walk in the Spirit, and you shall not fulfill the lust of the flesh"* (Gal. 5:16). How do we walk in the Spirit? Some argue that walking in the Spirit is regulating one's life by the rule/direction of the Holy Spirit. Galatians 5:25 says *"let us also walk in the Spirit."* The Greek word translated "walk" in verse 25 means to "walk in line." The Holy Spirit gives believers the rule, the direction by which to order their life. This is done through the Word of God, which the Spirit of God inspired. In Galatians 5, that rule/direction is love.

As we deal with our sin, do the Will of God and depend on the Holy Spirit, God is able to do His work in us and grow us to maturity.

Galatians 5:16 states *"I say then: Walk in the Spirit, and you shall not fulfill the lust of the flesh."* It is clear, if you are depending on the Spirit of God to work within you not even your fleshly desires will be able to control you.

SUMMARY

The Holy Spirit is the One that ultimately does the work in you as you apply the Word of God to your life daily. You must be faithful to obey and bring His Word into your life and you must ask Him to work as well. Remember that God is Sovereign and works in His time, His ways, and for His reasons.

nineteen

TRANSFORMATION

Transformation is the result of what God is doing in your life. As you experience the renovation (renewing) of your mind through the work of the Holy Spirit, transformation takes place within. Transformation is *not* something that *you do*, it is something that *happens to you*.

The word "transformation" appears only twice in the New Testament; Romans 12:2 and 2 Corinthians 3:18. You will recognize the Greek word translated "transform" is *metamorphoo* from which we get the word *metamorphose*. According to Strong's Hebrew and Greek Dictionary, this word means *to change to a different pattern, to change into a wholly different form or appearance*.

God has given us an example of transformation in nature. Every butterfly begins life as a caterpillar, goes through a *transformation,* and becomes a completely different life form. This is what every believer is to experience.

The Greek word translated *be transformed* is in the present passive imperative form. Being in the *imperative* mode means it is a command. It is in the *passive* voice which means that the action of the verb is done to the Christian. What this means is that God gives us a command and then He is the one that causes it to happen through the work of the Holy Spirit.

You obey His Word by depending upon His Spirit and He does the work to transform you into the image of His Son. The present tense also means that it is happening continuously. So you are being continuously transformed by the work of the Holy Spirit.

The Holy Spirit is the One that ultimately does the work in you. You are to be faithful to obey and bring His Word into your life and ask Him to work in you.

SUMMARY

As Christians, we are transformed into the image of Christ as we obey His Word through the power of the Holy Spirit.

twenty

LET GOD BE GOD

God operates on a different level so it is always best to accept God's ways even when we can't comprehend or understand what is happening. God sees tomorrow, we cannot see past right now. Isaiah 55:8-9 tells us why we should let God be God:

ISAIAH 55:8-9
For my thoughts are not your thoughts, neither are your ways my ways, declares the Lord. For as the heavens are higher than the earth, so are my ways higher than your ways and my thoughts than your thoughts.

Many Christians allow God to mold and shape them by submitting to the difficulties they experience, regardless of how painful they may be. Many learn the goodness and grace of God by responding appropriately and have found that God's grace is sufficient, regardless of circumstances.

My brother's mobility was suddenly taken from him by an abscess on his spinal cord. After a few months had passed I asked him, "How are you doing... really"? I was wanting to see how he was dealing with his loss. His response was immediate, "It is a privilege to suffer." He said it had never occurred to him to be upset. He accepted it as from God and immediately began working on learning to walk again. He was told that he would never walk again, however after nearly four years of hard work, he can walk without the use of a cane (although he does use one). He responded correctly and God blessed him.

When life throws you a curve and you are overwhelmed, remember that God is doing this *for* you whether He answers your prayers or not. If He doesn't get you out of the trial, it is because He wants to sustain you *in* and *through* the trial. A colleague of mine was going through a very difficult time in his life. He told me that he prayed that the Lord would not remove the issue until he had learned what God was teaching him. That's ultimately the heart attitude that God wants you to take.

HABAKKUK

When Habakkuk surveyed the situation in Israel, he saw the sin of the people and the silence of God. His prayer is recorded in Hab. 1:2-4:

HABAKKUK 1:2-4
O LORD, how long shall I cry, And You will not hear? Even cry out to You, 'Violence!' And You will not save. Why do You show me iniquity, and cause me to see trouble? For plundering and violence are before me; there is strife, and contention arises. Therefore the law is powerless, and justice never goes forth. For the wicked surround the righteous; therefore perverse judgment proceeds.

Habakkuk saw iniquity, injustice and the inactivity of God. The sins he saw included violence, strife and contention. What troubled him most was that God was not doing anything. When people get upset at what God is doing or not doing they often get angry and run *from* the Lord. Habakkuk took his complaint *to* the Lord.

God informed His servant that He was doing something. He told Habakkuk to *"Look among the nations and watch—be utterly astounded! For I will work a work in your days which you would not believe, though it were told you"* (Hab. 1:2-5). God was raising up the Babylonians to discipline Israel. Habakkuk could not see it but God was working. God's message to Habakkuk and to us is, "Trust Me. I am working whether you think so or not."

JOB

Things happen that we do not understand. Sometimes we feel that God is unjust in allowing the events of our life. Job felt that way and he spoke to God to voice his disapproval of what was happening.

Gain a perspective on *who* God is in His answer to Job, recorded in Job 38 to 41. Actually, God did not answer Job's question. Instead, God threw more than 70 questions at him so that Job would understand that God is God. Beginning with Job 38:2, *"Who is thiss who darkens counsel by words without knowledge?"* God continues with Job 38:4, *"Where were you when I laid the foundations of the earth?"* In 42:6 Job understood and said, *"I abhor myself, and repent in dust and ashes."*

THE BEST IS YET TO COME

This truth is illustrated in a story about an elderly woman who was told by her physician that she probably wouldn't live much longer. She gathered her family to discuss her funeral arrangements. They talked about how the service would be, where she would be buried, what kind of casket would be used, etc. As the conversation was winding down, the woman remarked, "There's one thing that's very important to me. I want to be buried with a fork in my right hand." Her children were understandably puzzled by that remark and one of them couldn't contain his curiosity. "Mom," he said, "What are you talking about?"

She said, "I remember eating with my family when I was a young girl and each of us would help clear away the dishes. Every once in a while, mom would tell us, 'Save your fork!' We knew what that meant. It meant that mom had fixed us a pie or a cake or some sort of treat. When she said 'Save your fork!,' that meant the best was yet to come. So I want to be buried with a fork in my hand, for the best is yet to come!"

THE PRESENT IS TEMPORARY

Take the perspective that the pain and suffering of this present world is only temporary and the best is yet to come.

> **ROMANS 8:18**
> *For I consider that the sufferings of this present time are not worthy to be compared with the glory which shall be revealed in us.*

GOD IS RIGHT

God is always right in what He does in and through your life. He alone knows what is best for you. You are on this earth for a reason. Learn of His grace and His power *in* your circumstances. Chuck Swindoll said, *"We're all faced with a series of great opportunities brilliantly disguised as impossible situations."*

Allow God to use your current circumstance to conform you into the image of His Son. When Paul understood this, he was glad for the difficulties. James said to count it all joy when you are in trials because it will produce in you maturity. Does God understand your pain and suffering? Yes.

> **HEBREWS 12:11**
> *No discipline seems pleasant at the time, but painful. Later on, however,*

it produces a harvest of righteousness and peace for those who have been trained by it.

Once again, He is giving us the reason why we experience difficulties in this life; to produce a harvest of righteousness and peace. God understands that what you are going through is painful and He wants you to know that He is going to produce righteousness and peace in you.

Paul, James, and the writer of Hebrews all are saying the same thing. Whatever is happening is happening for a reason; so that God can demonstrate His grace in you and bring you to maturity in Christ.

SUMMARY

Let God be God!

twenty-one

CONCLUSION

I have addressed three common reasons why Christians seek counseling and offered Biblical answers. I placed them in the three categories of trials, relationships, and mental disorders. I discussed how to live the Spiritual life. By so doing you will not have the difficulties discussed in this book.

TRIALS

Trials come into the life of a Christian to conform him or her into the image of His Son (Romans 8:28-29). When we fail to involve God in our trials we become anxious (Philippians 4:6-7), angry (James 1:19-20), or depressed (Jonah 4:1-11). We are to view our trials with calm delight (James 1:2) because God is at work conforming us into His Son's image. We are to be patient, endure the trial, and allow it to produce in us maturity (James 1:3-4). If you don't handle trials Biblically you may become bitter and have a negative influence on others (Hebrews 12:11-15).

RELATIONSHIPS

In regards to relationships we are to treat each other the way God treats us. He loves us unconditionally (1 Corinthians 13:4-8), forgives us freely (Ephesians 4:32), and He shows us grace every chance he gets (Mark 14: 66-72). To restore a damaged relationship, never argue (Proverbs 17:14) *and* practice how love behaves (1 Corinthians 13: 4-8).

MENTAL DISORDERS

As far as mental disorders are concerned, genetics, a chemical imbalance, or environmental influences are considered the cause or contributors to maladaptive or extreme behavior. Since these issues do not survive close examination we are left to explain that behavior, even maladaptive or extreme behavior, is the result of the individual's lack of self-control in the choices they make. Choice is the Biblical view of behavior.

THE SPIRITUAL LIFE

Man's problem began in the Garden of Eden when Adam and Eve disobeyed God's clear and direct command. Every problem that we have is directly related to sin that entered the human race after Adam and Eve disobeyed God.

The only way to have peace is to live the Spiritual Life as God intended. We are to be doers of the Word and not just hearers only (James 1:22). As we cooperate with the Holy Spirit by doing what God said, He transforms us into the image of Jesus Christ.

The purpose of this book is to encourage you to accept that God is conforming you into the Image of His Son. This is accomplished through trials, learning to treat people the same way that God treats you and practicing self-control in every area of your life.

A kindergarten teacher had all the children draw a picture and then tell a story about what they had drawn. As the teacher eased around the room to observe what was being drawn, one little girl's picture caught her attention. "What are you drawing?" asked the teacher. The little girl responded, "I'm drawing a picture of God." The teacher said, "Sweetie, no one knows what God looks like." Quickly, the little girl said, "They will in just a minute!"

God wants to draw a picture with your life so others will know what He looks like. May God richly bless you as you cooperate with the work of the Holy Spirit and apply His Word to your daily life.

the author

JOHN T. COCORIS

John T. Cocoris has devoted his life since the early 1970's to developing the temperament model of behavior. John has a B.A. from Tennessee Temple University, a Masters of Theology (Th. M.) from Dallas Theological Seminary, a Masters in Counseling (M.A.) from Amberton University and a Doctorate in Psychology (Psy. D.) from California Coast University. John is a licensed counselor in the state of Texas.

John established Profile Dynamics in the early 1980's to develop and promote the temperament model of behavior for use in business and counseling. He has been a management consultant since 1984 and has worked with a variety of companies giving seminars for training managers and sales people. John has been interviewed on the radio and has been featured numerous times on COPE, a national cable TV talk show.

John has written many books and manuals about the temperament model including: The Temperament Model of Behavior, Understanding Your Natural Tendencies; Born With A Creative Temperament, The Sanguine-Melancholy (I/C); 7 Steps To A Better You, How To Develop Your Natural Tendencies; Discover Your Child's Temperament, Born With Natural Tendencies; A Therapist's Guide to The Temperament Model of Behavior; How to Supervise Others Using The Temperament Model of Behavior; Effective Selling Using The Temperament Model of Behavior; The DISC II Temperament Assessment; The DISC II Temperament Assessment User Guide; DISC II Library, 15 Pattern Series; The DISC 3 Temperament Assessment; The DISC 3 Temperament Assessment User Guide.

references

references

JOHN T. COCORIS

Breggin, P. R. (1994). *Toxic psychiatry: Why therapy, empathy and love must replace the drugs, electroshock, and biochemical theories of the "new psychiatry".* New York, NY: St. Martin's Press.

Breggin, P. R. (2012). Do you have a biochemical imbalance? [Episode 1] *Simple truths about psychology.* Podcast retrieved from http://breggin.com/index.php?option=com_content&task=view&id=297&Itemid=130

Breggin, P. R., & Cohen, D. (1999). *Your drug may be your problem: How and why to stop taking psychiatric medications.* Philadelphia, PA: Da Capo Press.

Carver, J. (2009). *The chemical imbalance in mental health problems.* Retrieved from http://mental-health-matters.com/the-chemical-imbalance-in-mental-health-problems/2/

Cocoris, J. T. (2014). *The temperament model of behavior: Understanding your natural tendencies.* McKinney, TX: Profile Dynamics.

Cocoris, M. (n.d.). *The spiritual life, clarifying the confusion about being conformed into the image of Christ.* New York, NY: St. Martin's Press.

Cocoris, M. (n.d.). Notes on Hebrews 12:15.

Cocoris, M. (n.d). Notes on Proverbs 3:5-6.

Constable, T. L. (2015). The character of love 13:4-7. In *Notes on 1 Corinthians.* Retrieved from http://www.soniclight.com/constable/notes/htm/NT/1%20Corinthians/1Corinthians.htm

Constable, T. L. (2015). The end product of trials 1:3-4. In *Notes on James*. Retrieved from http://www.soniclight.com/constable/notes/htm/NT/James/James.htm

Constable, T. L. (2015). The permanence of love 13:8-13. In *Notes on 1 Corinthians*. Retrieved from http://www.soniclight.com/constable/notes/htm/NT/1%20Corinthians/1Corinthians.htm

Constable, T. L. (2015). Judah's indelible sin and sin's deceitfulness 17:1-18. In *Notes on Jeremiah*. Retrieved from http://www.soniclight.com/constable/notes/htm/OT/Jeremiah/Jeremiah.htm

Dalrymple, T. (2013). Bad behavior isn't an illness. *Los Angeles Times*. Retrieved from http://articles.latimes.com/2013/nov/05/opinion/la-oe-dalrymple-dsm-diseases-20131105

Evans, R. L. (1969). In the year 2525. [Recorded by Zager & Evans]. On *In the year 2525 (Exordium et Terminus)*. [CD]. Texas: RCA Victor.

Glasser, W. (1984). *Take effective control of your life*. New York, NY: Harper Collins.

Glasser, W. (2004). *Warning: Psychiatry can be hazardous to your mental health*. New York, NY: Harper Perennial.

Kraus, M. W. (2013). Do genes influence personality? A summary of recent advances in the nature vs. nurture debate. *Under the influence*. Retrieved from https://www.psychologytoday.com/blog/under-the-influence/201307/do-genes-influence-personality

Maugh II, T. H., (2012). Dr. Thomas Szasz dies at 92; psychiatrist who attacked profession. *Los Angeles Times*. Retrieved from http://articles.latimes.com/2012/sep/17/local/la-me-thomas-szasz-20120917-1

National Alliance on Mental Illness. (2015). What is mental illness. *Mental illnesses*. Retrieved from http://www2.nami.org/Content/NavigationMenu/Inform_Yourself/About_Mental_Illness/By_Illness/What_is_Mental_Illness_.htm

(n.d.). *What does it mean to lean not on your own understanding*. Retrieved from http://www.gotquestions.org/lean-not-own-understanding.html

Ross, C., & Pam, A. (1995). *Pseudoscience in biological psychiatry: Blaming the body.* New York, NY: John Wiley & Sons, Inc.

Schwartz, A. (2014). Idea of new attention deficit disorder spurs research, and debate. *New York Times.* Retrieved from http://www.nytimes.com/2014/04/12/health/idea-of-new-attention-disorder-spurs-research-and-debate.html?_r=0

Watts, I. (1707). When I survey the wondrous cross.

WebMD. (2015). What causes mental illness? *Mental Illness Basics.* Retrieved from http://www.webmd.com/mental-health/mental-illness-basics.

www.ingramcontent.com/pod-product-compliance
Lightning Source LLC
Chambersburg PA
CBHW050555300426
44112CB00013B/1924